Coaching in Organisations:

Between the Lines

KERI PHILLIPS

Published by: Claremont Management Consultants Ltd

Copyright © Claremont Management Consultants Ltd

Designed and Produced by Qwertyop, The Vatch, Slad, Glos. GL6 7JY

All rights reserved. No part of the book may be reprinted or reproduced or utilised in any form or by any electronic, mechanical or other means, now known or hereafter invented, including photocopying and recording, or in any information storage or retrieval system, without the permission in writing from the Publisher..

British Library Cataloguing in Publication Data.
A catalogue record of this book is available from the British Library.

ISBN 0-9536339-1-8

DEDICATION

To Freda and Phil

contents

page no.

PREFACE ... iv

Chapter One: INTRODUCTION ... 1
Why are we writing this?
About this book

Chapter Two: THE CONTENT AND PROCESS OF COACHING ... 7
Defining terms
The context for coaching
The domains of coaching
The coaching journey
Some likely questions on the coaching journey

Chapter Three: STORIES ... 27
Coach on the couch
The coachee speaks

Chapter Four: SOME COMMON PITFALLS ... 43
Collusion with the coachee
Over-reliance on objectives
Lack of variety in approach
Performing/trying to look clever
Over-investment in the coachee making changes
Unrealistic expectations of self and coachee
Failure to re-contract

Chapter Five: PERSPECTIVES - THE COACH'S MANAGER ... 51
Balancing involvement and detachment
Developing coaches as individuals and a team

page no.

Chapter Six: PERSPECTIVES - THE COACHEE'S MANAGER   59
- Line manager as coach?
- Raising the need for coaching
- Contributor to a learning organisation – the influence of the environment
- Contributor to a learning organisation – learning to learn

Chapter Seven: PERSPECTIVES - THE SPONSOR   71

Chapter Eight: CONCLUSION   79

APPENDICES   83

One:	The contract in coaching
Two:	A framework for session management
Three:	Suggested guidelines for the coachee
Four:	Tools and techniques
Five:	Suggested ethical guidelines for the coach
Six:	Annotated bibliography
Seven:	Useful contacts

FINAL THOUGHT   99

TABLE OF FIGURES

Figure one	Positioning coaching	9
Figure two	Domains of coaching	12
Figure two (a)	Widening the scope	13
Figure two (b)	Narrowing the scope	13
Figure three	Coaching boundaries	14
Figure four	The coachee's journey	17
Figure five	The coach's journey	18
Figure six	Attitudes to coaching	64
Figure seven	Content and process coaching	67
Figure eight	Focus of sponsorship in coaching	72
Figure nine	Issues for coach and sponsor	75
Figure ten	Creating positive change	80

Preface

Why are we bothering to write and publish yet another book on the subject of coaching? Surely there are many, many books that cover this topic? In fact, this book is the first in a series of topics of interest to managers that we are intending to publish. Why are we, a small management consultancy that specialises in organisation development, bothering to do this?

There are some very good books on coaching and we list several in appendix six. However, as consultants with quite a lot of coaching experience behind us, we feel that many of these books, whilst giving a good grounding in tools and techniques, sometimes do not want to scare you by telling you how potentially difficult coaching is and what pitfalls you might encounter.

Some of these pitfalls come through sticking too closely to commonly-held views as to the 'do's and don'ts' of coaching methods. For example, most approaches emphasise the importance of not giving direct advice to the client. However, there are times when clear, direct feedback and advice is just what is required. Another example focuses on the conventional wisdom that it is always helpful to encourage the client to set clear goals; and yet, for some people whose life has been driven by 'doing' rather than 'being', the opposite might be true.

Other difficulties can come as a result of not thinking through the wider organisational implications of the coaching process and understanding the role of other stakeholders outside the coaching room, such as the coach's manager and the human resources department. Yet others arise with a failure to recognise that the coach is not a totally objective, rational, 'sorted' person, but brings his or her own needs and blind spots to the coaching situation.

So, this book is designed to explore the things about coaching they do not necessarily teach you on courses and that only come through finding out the hard way. We do not cover the basic methods, but we do explore, hopefully, in a new way how to make coaching really work.

This book is written in part for experienced coaches who want a perspective on the nuances, dilemmas and anxieties of coaching for real. It is also written for those who set up coaching processes in organisations, to help them consider how to make the initiatives even more successful.

Keri Phillips is the author of this book. I have worked with Keri for ten years or so and this writing reflects his qualities. It is based in part on conversations with others, coachees, coaches, and clients, and contains the wisdom and experience of many. As always, Keri brings a creative and challenging perspective to the material and presents new models and approaches for us to consider. For example, he makes the point that coaching should not just help us to make decisions or learn new skills, but should also help us to reflect more generally on the ways we, as individuals, build theories, learn and change. In this way we can learn to be our own coaches. I had never thought of it in that way before. Equally, have you ever considered all the ways coaching can be established in your business and what are the pros and cons of each approach? You will find such material in this book.

It is a short book; it is not entirely polished and complete. It is different, sometimes challenging and occasionally difficult. We hope you dip into it as a resource and let some of the real-life stories and models rattle around a bit and see where they take you. And, we hope you contact us to challenge us and perhaps disagree with our points of view!

Thank you Keri, for putting, as always, your heart and soul into this project.

Jean Boulton
Managing Director
Claremont Management Consultants Ltd
Bath

January 2004

Email: jeanboulton@claremont-mc.co.uk
Website: www.claremont-mc.co.uk

chapter one

Introduction

WHY ARE WE WRITING THIS?

This book has been written for those who are directly involved in coaching in organisations and those who are simply interested in a subject that is of growing topicality, as shown by the fact that it spawns an increasingly vast array of publications. It is, therefore, aimed at the coach, the coachee and those who are considering establishing a coaching process as an organisational intervention. With this in mind, we are acutely aware at Claremont that, in adding to that pile, we have to be clear about what we seek to offer.

During the years of our participation in coaching initiatives we have increasingly recognised that they are frequently multi-faceted projects; in other words, there is a lot more to coaching than might initially be apparent. So, along with some of the accolades, we can recall those situations where we scratched our heads, wondering where we were going wrong. Sometimes we found out, sometimes we were left guessing. This book, therefore, has been written to share some of our insights and our unresolved questions from what has been a fascinating, sometimes bumpy, journey.

In this publication we look at coaching from the perspective of the key figures who might well be taking part, and offer a blend of theory, 'campfire' stories and practical tips. It is not intended to be a step-by-step guide; there are already many publications which offer this, as set out in appendix six. Rather this is something of a personal statement based on the themes, understandings and confusions which have arisen for us. On those rare occasions where we offer 'truths' and certainties, we do so recognising that they are probably temporary, and may well be called into question by next year's (or even next week's) assignment. We invite the reader to contact us to further the debate, perhaps taking some mischievous but ultimately productive pleasure in pointing out to us where we err in our exposition.

Certainly the idea of coaching often seems to need some explanation in the business world; this does not seem to be the case in the world of sport. This may on occasion be due to some inherent confusion as to the nature of coaching. It may be that the coaching being undertaken is challenging some basic assumptions within a particular organisation; for example, in some organisations, asking for help is seen as a sign of weakness. So sometimes there is an education phase needed in organisations about what can be realistically expected and the responsibilities of those involved; only after this can the coaching begin in earnest. We hope that our book will assist in this.

ABOUT THIS BOOK

As we are at pains to make clear, this book does not set out to teach the basic methods and techniques of the coaching conversation. Rather, we are seeking to look at the issues both in and around coaching that perhaps receive less attention; we think they are, nevertheless, vital for success, both at an individual and organisational level.

In chapter two we map out the territory of coaching. What is it and what is it not? In what ways can coaching be tackled in an organisation? When might internal rather than external coaches be used and what are the pros and cons? Would it be a good idea to connect coaching with performance management or not?

We also look at the stages of the coaching process, from the perspectives of both coach and coachee. We touch on the point that the coach inevitably brings his own needs, wounds and strong views no matter how much he tries to be an objective, empty vessel. We look at some of the questions and dilemmas that arise on the way. What is success? How does the coach know when it is time to end the coaching process? What might the coach do when starting to feel out of his depth?

We move on in chapter three to some very direct and personal experiences of both coaches and coachees. These are all real situations drawn from our colleagues and clients. We asked these people to give us stories which captured key learning, memorable events, delights and difficulties. As such, they give a flavour of 'coaching for real', and highlight some of the potential obstacles. For example, the coach may not consider that by not leaving enough time between sessions, coachees may bump into each other. In certain coaching situations this risks a loss of privacy, as well as perhaps allowing each coachee to feel more of a number than a name. In another instance, one story we include highlights the question of how to handle the situation where the coachee raises a concern, in this example loss of contact with his children, which may resonate with the coach's own personal history. These stories allow us to grapple with some of the real-life situations we may meet as coachees and coaches. Hopefully, they will give us clues on handling such situations if we meet them ourselves.

In chapter four, we try to summarise and synthesise some of the common, yet less obvious 'traps' into which the coach can stumble. We challenge, perhaps, some of the established wisdom of coaching in so doing. For example, is it always right to help the coachee set objectives? Do we get too caught up in trying to look good ourselves? When is it helpful to say we were wrong or that we do not know the answer to something? When should we walk away from a potential piece of coaching work? Under what circumstances should we quit?

The next three chapters describe the challenges, options and responsibilities faced by those who may well be key figures in any coaching initiative: the manager of the coach or coaches (chapter five), the line manager of the coachee (chapter six) and the sponsor of the whole coaching enterprise; that is, the person who puts their authority behind it (chapter seven). The diagram below shows the most common positioning of these roles.

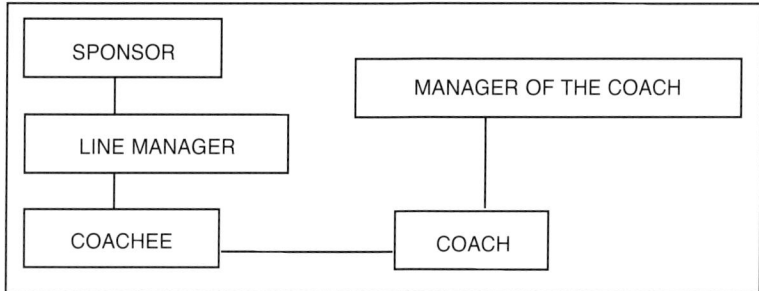

In our experience, the wisdom, expectations and behaviour of these three characters, and the awareness of their importance by the coach, can make or break coaching initiatives. Is the manager of the coach trying to sell more work or build alliances when she, perhaps, needs to be totally objective and free from her own agenda in order best to support the process? What happens if the sponsor, in launching a so-called coaching initiative, then seeks to use it as a cloak-and-dagger assessment process? How does the line manager undermine the process and how could he be more supportive? How much contact should the coach have with him? We will explore issues such as these in these three chapters.

Following the concluding chapter, chapter eight, there are seven appendices, each summarising what we regard as crucial information in a number of areas. These include how to 'contract' with the client for coaching, how to manage a coaching session and how to set ethical guidelines for the coach. There are also guidelines for the coachee so that he or she can get the best out of the process and take the right level of responsibility. We also include an annotated bibliography and list useful contacts in the world of coaching. These appendices are designed as stand-alone checklists and guidance, so they can be used, if required, separately from the book.

So, let us move onto the core of the book. We start with 'the content and process of coaching'.

Introduction

*Only by holding the coachee
with an open hand
can the coach be
truly supportive*

chapter two

The content and process of coaching

This chapter has been written to present an overview of coaching both in terms of the content of what is discussed and the process, that is, the ways in which coaching can take place. We concentrate first on defining terms, taking into account the many and varied interpretations of coaching and other related developmental activities. Secondly, we outline some of the variables which can affect the context for coaching, recognising that it can have many formats. For example, an organisation's style in its approach to coaching may be to use external consultants extensively; in contrast, the organisation may expect the coaching to be carried out solely by members of staff.

Thirdly, we look broadly at the likely focus of the coaching, in terms of the range of coachee issues which might be brought forward for consideration. We use the word 'domains' for this, examining the possible matches and mismatches between coachee need and the coach's choice of intervention. Fourthly, we examine the likely phases of coaching as experienced by both coach and coachee. At this stage we introduce the idea of the 'coaching journey'. We develop this further in the final part of this chapter when we consider some of the questions which can commonly arise for both coach and coachee on this journey.

DEFINING TERMS

In adding to the almost self-reproducing literature in this field we are under no illusion that what we offer below, in defining terms, will magically pull together and integrate the multiplicity of labels that already exists. All we can say is that this is how we have made some sense of things, developing a common language to help communication both between ourselves and our customers; it is still work in progress.

One of the difficulties seems to be that quite often, and probably not surprisingly, specialists in management development will have their favoured technique. When writing about it they tend to make it central and can sometimes seem to regard anything else as somewhat peripheral or a distortion or irrelevant. They then write definitions which are crafted to support an individualistic and sometimes idiosyncratic view of the world. For example, a recent book on mentoring chose to define coaching as mainly directive, with the learning process largely one way; that is to say, the book suggests it is essentially only the person being coached who learns. There are many management coaches who would howl with outrage at such a suggestion, and would want to emphasise that the process is inevitably, and appropriately, two-way.

Despite appearances to the contrary, we, in Claremont, are not claiming the moral high ground. We are simply saying that we have found a language that seems to work for us and our customers, as well as adding to the world's over supply of definitions of coaching, counselling, training and therapy! So, for the purposes of this book, here they are:

Training: A series of managed activities involving individuals and/or groups where a trainer seeks to help a trainee or trainees meet pre-determined objectives.

Coaching: A series of conversations, usually between two individuals, where one, the coach, seeks to help the other, the coachee, become more effective at work.

Counselling: A series of conversations between two individuals where one, the counsellor, seeks to help the other, the client, become more effective in handling personal and life concerns.

Therapy: A series of conversations between two individuals where one, the therapist, seeks to help the other, the client or patient, become more effective in handling some particularly profound personal and life concerns and relate these back to early childhood experiences.

We acknowledge that there is some oversimplification in these definitions, and that there are areas of overlap. Partially to meet these concerns we put these activities on a spectrum, as shown in figure one overleaf:

Figure one
Positioning coaching

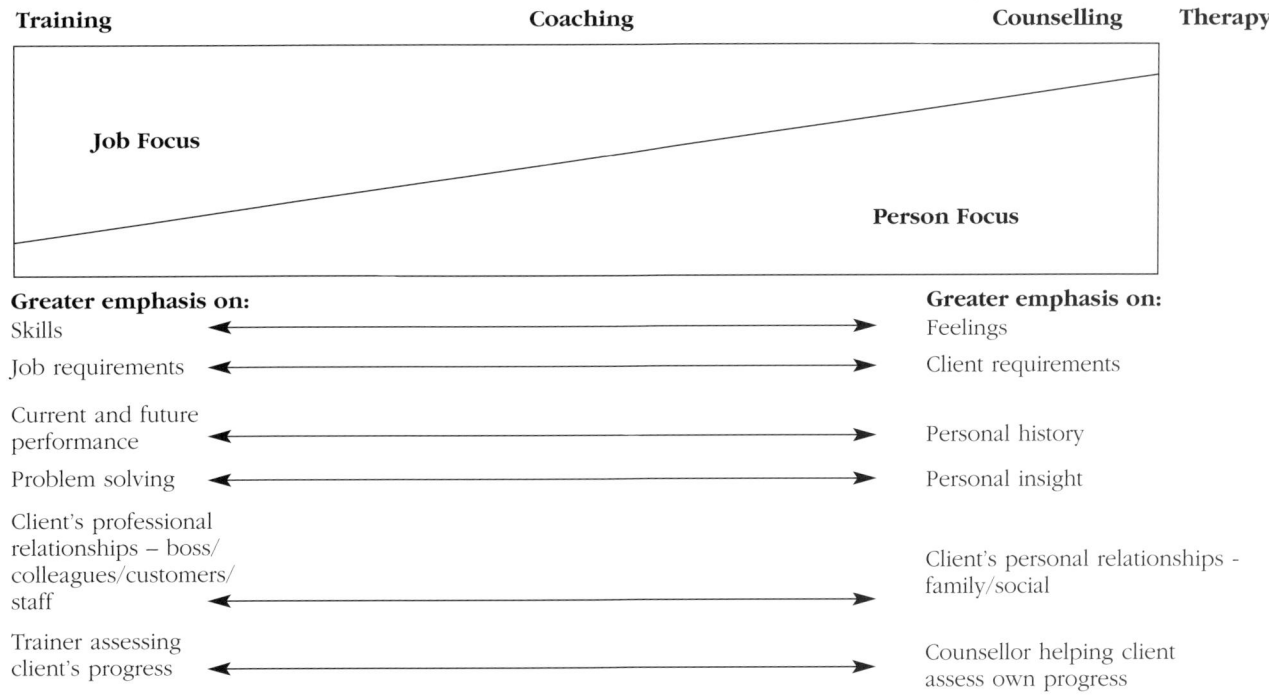

What this is intended to show is that coaching broadly holds a middle ground. This sometimes requires the coach to manage some tricky dilemmas. For example, the coachee will often present a mixture of work-related and personal concerns. The coach is then faced with the task of navigating through this rich landscape in a way which is neither inappropriately intrusive, nor ritualistically superficial.

A notable omission from the diagram is the role of mentor. We found that the mentor has so many, often quite different, manifestations (for example academic supervisor / sponsor / advocate / personal careers advisor) that we chose not to position it at all, even loosely. This is not intended, in any way, to downplay the contribution of mentoring in management and organisation development.

We have also left therapy 'hanging', to indicate that it does not, in our view, have a role in organisational life.

THE CONTEXT FOR COACHING

The formats for coaching vary a great deal. The most common ones of which we are aware are outlined below. Choosing a format has a significant impact on the process. For example, a decision as to whether it is the line manager, or someone else, who will be the coach is of vital importance. In considering these formats we are not suggesting that one choice is necessarily better than another, since there will usually be pros and cons to be evaluated. However, we would argue strongly for active and aware decisions in all these areas.

Internal/external coach. The internal coach may have a clearer understanding of the organisation's culture, the key players and ways of influencing the situation to support the coachee; equally, she may be too close to see it clearly. The external coach may, as an outsider be more readily trusted by the coachee, and not be seen as having a hidden agenda; but the external may naively misjudge the organisational politics. Our impression is that internal coaches are more likely to be used where specific skills are needed, externals being invited in when more sensitive and personal issues may be expected to arise.

One-off session or series or open-ended. One-off coaching sessions can be good for concentrating the minds of all parties; effectiveness will be dependent upon solid, advance preparation, establishing very clearly what is possible, as well as what is desirable in terms of outcomes.

Choosing a series of sessions, for example six, rather than a one-off, obviously allows much greater scope in examining a wider range of needs, some of which might only emerge as important over time; there is an opportunity for the coach and coachee to deepen their understanding of each other, and explore what, potentially, can be achieved and what are the underlying themes.

We define open-ended to mean that the coaching lasts as long as it takes. This carries with it many of the same advantages as the agreed series, but the possible disadvantages are mutual dependency, too great a convergence of view between coach and coachee and a lack of discipline in seeking solid outcomes. It also loses the effect of knowing that the process is coming to an end, which can often precipitate movement.

Linked/not linked to performance management processes. In our view, any good performance management (PM) process has coaching as a central feature. Coaching will be seen as a way of supporting the coachee in the meeting of his performance objectives. So PM can provide structure and rigour to coaching, but it may on occasion make the coaching too narrow in its focus. Equally, this could be argued as a failure of the way in which the PM is implemented rather than of the coaching process itself.

Coach is/is not the coachee's manager. This point is covered in more detail later, but here are some initial points. The manager is probably readily available to coach, perhaps in the light of noticing the coachee's behaviour in a particular situation. This may be especially relevant for job skills coaching. The line manager may have a very strong investment in the success of the coaching; this can be a mixed blessing as there might not be enough detachment and the coach might take the coachee's failure as a personal affront.

Coachee initiates/does not initiate the coaching. A statement of the obvious is that the coaching will have a much more positive start if the coachee makes the first move. If this does not happen, the line manager may need to offer feedback and other data to the coachee, to indicate inadequate performance. Part of the emphasis in a lot of PM initiatives has been the seeking to create a 'culture change' so that it becomes accepted in the organisation that people take responsibility for their development. Indeed the logic of the argument is that once such an attitude is second nature, then the formalities of 'process', whatever it might be, are scarcely needed.

Coaching as an informal/formal activity. Arguably most coaching in organisations is, and should be, informal. This might take the form of 'ad hoc' discussions, probably with the line manager as coach, whenever the need arises. It might not even look like coaching to the casual observer. A downside may be that a lack of time makes the ad hoc coaching too much about giving advice, rather than helping the coachee discover his own solutions. In contrast, the formal coaching carried out at pre-arranged times, by internal or external coaches, can allow time for the consideration of substantive and wider issues.

There is/is not a sponsor for coaching. If external coaches are used, there is likely to be a financial cost. There may well, though not inevitably, be an individual, senior to the line manager, who has to authorise expenditure and champion the activity. When there is such a person, then the coaching may be less solely focused on individual development, but be part of an organisation development initiative.

One-to-one versus group coaching. Generally coaching assumes just two people are taking part in the actual coaching itself. However, there does seem to be a growing trend towards the coaching of pairs – peers, or manager and staff member. Also there is the possibility of group coaching - for example, linked to development centres, action learning sets or team-building; this also can be part of an organisation development strategy.

Face-to-face or distance coaching. Advances in technology, as well an increased pressure on time, have led to more coaching taking place 'at a distance'. A 'mixed' approach seems common; it may include face-to-face meetings, with ongoing, interim support through telephone, e-mail and video link.

At the beginning of this section we mentioned the importance of making conscious decisions about these formats. Such decision-making is a way of ensuring that the coaching takes place in a way that matches the current needs of the organisation. Also, it vastly increases the chances that all those involved has clear expectations of the process and each other. The debate leading up to these decisions can help create a climate which is truly supportive of coaching whether for individual, team or organisation development, or all three.

THE DOMAINS OF COACHING

As already touched upon, the focus of coaching can vary considerably with a wide variety of emphasis. This might depend upon job requirements, the preoccupations of the coachee and indeed the interests and skills of the coach. We group this content into three areas, which we call domains, illustrating and describing them in figure two below:

Figure two
Domains of coaching

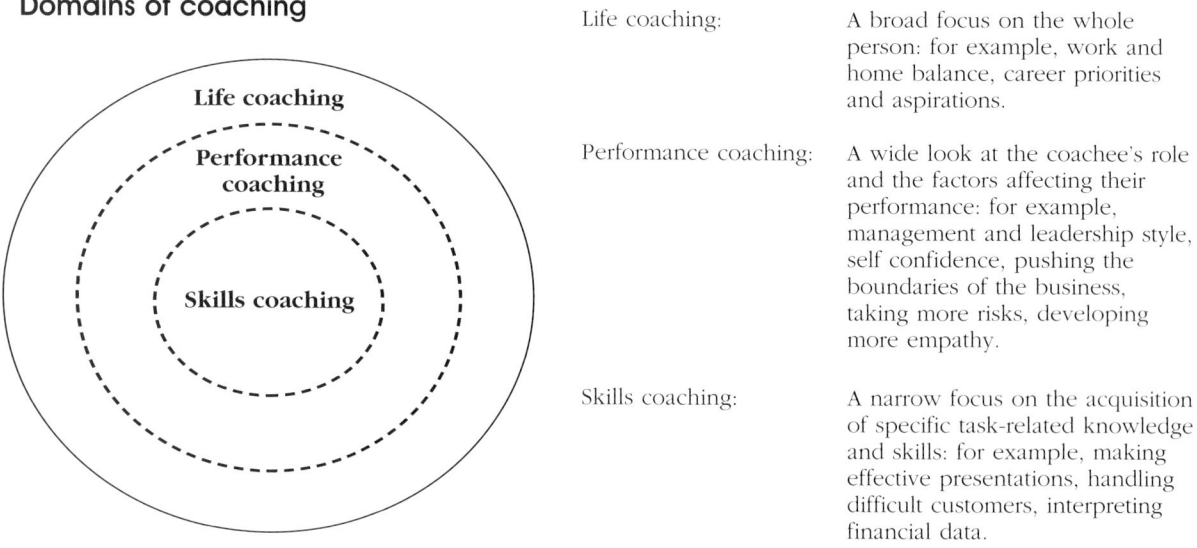

Life coaching: A broad focus on the whole person: for example, work and home balance, career priorities and aspirations.

Performance coaching: A wide look at the coachee's role and the factors affecting their performance: for example, management and leadership style, self confidence, pushing the boundaries of the business, taking more risks, developing more empathy.

Skills coaching: A narrow focus on the acquisition of specific task-related knowledge and skills: for example, making effective presentations, handling difficult customers, interpreting financial data.

We can also position these domains in relation to figure one, which sets coaching in a wider context. Skills coaching is more likely to take place towards the training end of the coaching spectrum, with life coaching more towards the counselling end.

We would suggest that the coach needs to be clear about her position on this spectrum, whether generally or for specific clients. This clarity establishes at the outset whether there is a likely match with the coachee's needs and expectations. Of course, the domains are not mutually exclusive and some movement between them is understandable. The skills coach might, for example, want to explore wider issues, as shown in figure two (a):

Equally, as shown on figure two (b), the life coach might want to narrow the focus and move closely into some specifics at work:

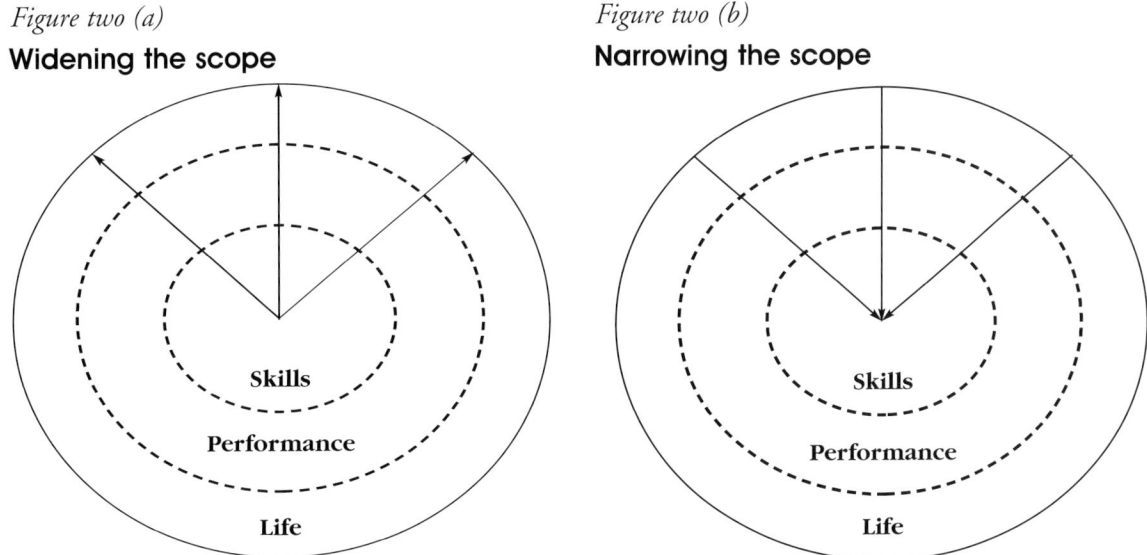

Figure two (a)
Widening the scope

Figure two (b)
Narrowing the scope

So, the life coach and the skills coach might overlap in their styles, although they will be coming from different directions.

Focus on the domains of coaching sheds light on the importance of contracting and regularly re-visiting the contract (see also appendix one). The coach, coachee and indeed sponsor may have very different expectations of where the emphasis of the work will take place. The coachee might be expecting to be coached on specific skills and then be affronted or excited at the prospect of wider issues being addressed. If the coaching considers broader life issues, then the question may be raised about how far this is relevant in terms of the coachee's job performance. This is a valid concern to be clarified, as is the closely-linked point about life coaching extending too far into personal issues which may be best dealt with by a qualified counsellor or therapist; so figure three indicates the need for this boundary.

Figure three
Coaching boundaries

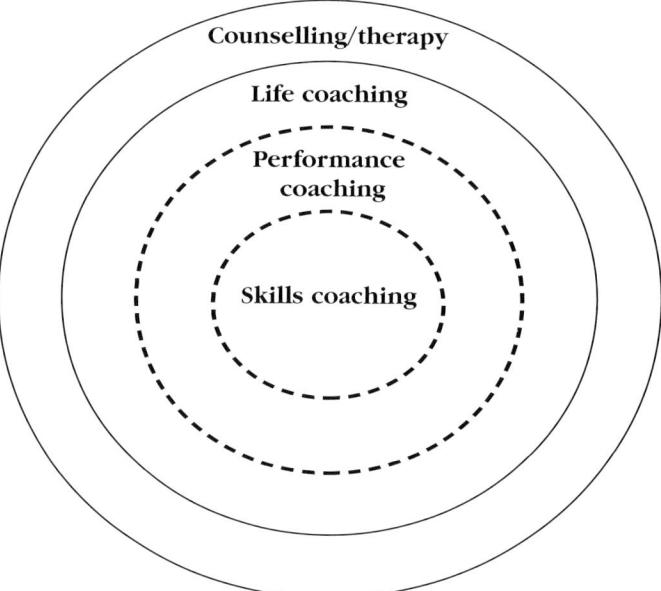

These boundaries for the coaching relationship are crucial since they will be frequently tested. There are many organisations where quality, in-depth listening is rare. When, therefore, the coachee is given the opportunity, she or he may well have a lot to talk about, quite possibly well beyond immediate job performance. A floodgate of feelings may be opened simply by the coach asking, *'what do you want to talk about?'*.

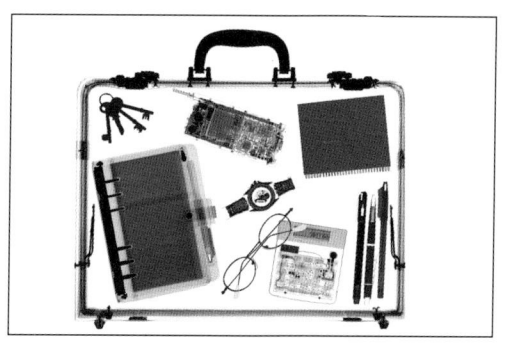

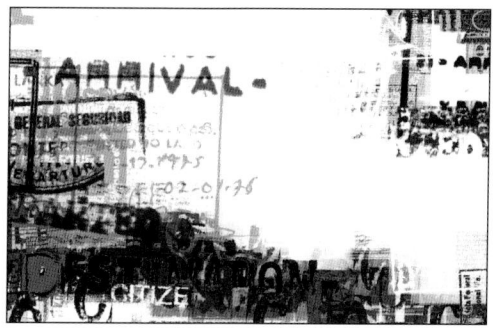

THE COACHING JOURNEY

Having considered the content aspect of coaching, we will now look at the coaching process itself. In the literature on coaching there are many descriptions of the likely phases in the lifetime of the coaching relationship. We draw together some of the most commonly suggested elements and term them 'journeys' for the coachee (figure four) and the coach (figure five). Then we consider some of the questions that might arise along the way. The fundamentals of the coaching process are not likely to be significantly affected whether the purpose of the coaching is developmental, making good performance even better, or remedial, raising performance to an acceptable level. There are several introductory points to make.

Stakeholders. First, in some coaching initiatives, as already touched on, there can be 'stakeholders' other than the coach and coachee to be considered. These are the 'sponsor', the person in the organisation who is, through money or authority, mandating the coaching; human resources, who may or may not be the sponsor; the coachee's line manager, unless this person is also the coach; and the coach's manager, particularly if the coach comes from an external consultancy or other provider.

So, sometimes the early stages of the coaching relationship are less an intimate tête-à-tête, rather a French farce with the various people sticking their heads round doors to declare an interest, or trying to hide under the bed! Obviously the more people that are involved, the more complex the contracting and, for example, the greater the challenges in establishing and agreeing confidentiality.

Progress is non-linear. Secondly, as can be inferred from the previous point, progress is rarely linear. Even when just two people are involved there will frequently be a need to re-visit previous stages, which were assumed to have been resolved. It is important to see this as progress, even if it does not feel like it at the time; commitment or trust are being properly tested, plans are being revised in the light of new information, previously unnoticed vagueness is being put under the spotlight. This iterative element also applies to session management, as described in appendix two.

Feelings. Thirdly, we fully recognise that there will be feelings such as excitement, anxiety, relief, confusion and delight for both parties at all stages of the journey. These will vary greatly in intensity, needing to be acknowledged by the coach either directly, *'what do you feel about this possible course of action?'*, or indirectly, by creating a physically – comfortable coaching environment. How intensely a coachee may feel about certain issues can be a surprise. For example, a decision to change career may for one coachee be emotionally charged; for another it might be quite low key since it feels such a natural next step.

The content and process of coaching

Figure four
The coachee's journey

Re-visiting dissatisfaction with own performance – honestly assessing progress.

Being honest with self about consequences – gathering information on the results; acknowledging successes and failures.

Mustering the courage to choose and take action – drawing on own personal reserves.

Being open to options – truly listening to possibilities; creating own ideas.

Finding the motivation to change – generating the energy to do something different.

Taking responsibility – accepting that change has to start with self.

Feeling dissatisfaction with own performance – receiving enough information, perhaps from various sources, to decide there is room for improvement.

Figure five

The coach's journey

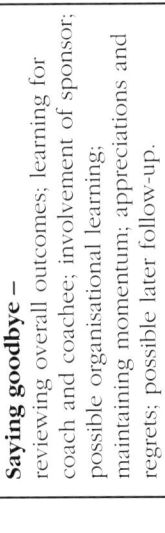

Saying goodbye – reviewing overall outcomes; learning for coach and coachee; involvement of sponsor; possible organisational learning; maintaining momentum; appreciations and regrets; possible later follow-up.

Travelling together – getting a clearer sense of the territory – areas to be considered, possible outcomes, establishing priorities, agreeing actions; reviewing support; identifying outcomes/learning; developing new perspectives/options; re-contracting, celebrating success.

Establishing common ground – exchanging expectations and initial wants; administration: frequency, length, number of meetings; confidentiality; nature of support between meetings; feedback – type, from whom to whom; contracting.

Saying hello to the coachee – establishing rapport; exploring motivation (did coachee initiate?) exchanging basic background information: role, experience, qualifications.

Saying hello to the sponsor – establishing the need and expectations; agreeing costs and confidentiality; contracting.

The content and process of coaching

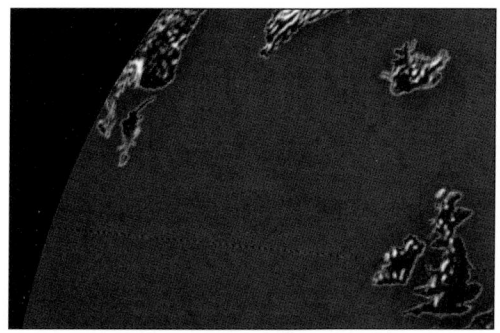

On their respective journeys both coach and coachee need to recognise their 'togetherness' and 'separateness', which are necessary features for successful coaching. The togetherness is based upon a willingness for both parties to invest time and trust in each other. The separateness is based upon two fundamental truths. First, that ultimately change can only come from within a person; the coachee himself is the only one who can make real decisions about new directions. Secondly, that sooner or later their paths must diverge. Of course, in all this both the coach and coachee each has his own unique and highly personal understanding of what togetherness and separateness means. This creates a fascinating dynamic, which we begin to consider in the next section, 'Some likely questions on the coaching journey'.

SOME LIKELY QUESTIONS ON THE COACHING JOURNEY

Below we describe some of the questions that, in our experience, commonly arise on the coaching journey. Just like a journey, the terrain for coaching can be easy or difficult; there can be false dawns; there may be the need to recuperate and there could be doubts about whether the right route has been chosen. It is also trite, but true, to say that the journey itself is as important as the destination. For example, learning how to handle false dawns is valuable in most aspects of business, and indeed in personal life. We use these questions to begin focusing on the realities and practicalities of coaching as well as suggesting possible actions.

Do we really agree on the destination?

When thinking about the coaching journey it is possible to be a little naïve. We might believe that the coach and coachee get together, agree the destination (for example, metaphorically, Worthing), get the map out, and head off in the right direction (south on the A24). However, one of the early challenges may be that the coachee is not necessarily motivated to go to Worthing. Perhaps it is her line manager, or the sponsor who says that she should go. It may be that the coachee is not profoundly opposed to going to Worthing, but wants more information wondering why Brighton is not an equally valid choice.

Under these circumstances the coach and coachee may need to decide whether they have enough information even to begin the journey. It is possible that the line manager has not sufficiently or clearly challenged the coachee's performance, not offering enough evidence on where improvements need to be made. It may be that the line manager allowed himself to get swept along by the sponsor's enthusiasm.

All this points to some important conversations between all these parties as to why coaching might be needed. It may even be a matter of revisiting earlier conversations where it had appeared that these issues had been resolved. For example, it was, perhaps, only after the coaching had started that the line manager's lack of support became apparent.

As a reaction against these uncertainties, the coach can be tempted to go to the opposite extreme, wanting certainty on everything (the house number and street in Worthing). With life, performance and possibly even skills coaching, it may well not be possible or even desirable that there is such specificity early in the coaching process. The coach may be better advised to look for commitment to going on a journey with a rough destination in mind (somewhere on the South coast), with the end point being firmed up later. The best destination can sometimes only be decided once the journey has begun. For example, in terms of developing trust, the coachee might metaphorically want to wander with the coach round the shops in Dorking for a few hours before deciding whether to embark on a rather more ambitious journey!

Do we know whether we are on the right route?

There are several facets to this question. The coach and coachee may see very clearly the progress that has been made. For example, this could mean the coachee is displaying renewed confidence in handling meetings with staff, or an improvement in customer satisfaction ratings, or has passed exams, or has shown a new ability to analyse and interpret spreadsheets. Following our analogy, both parties can stand on a hill and have an uninterrupted view of the path travelled so far and what lies ahead – it is a clear day on the South Downs.

Doubts are part of learning. However, the coachee may have doubts about progress, ranging from slight unease to deep disquiet. From the coach's point of view it is important, despite the temptation, not to over-react to these concerns, whilst obviously taking them seriously. For example, it is possible that the coachee's feelings are a natural part of learning. It might be that she is in a 'no man's land' where some old behaviour has been relinquished, such as being passive when unfairly criticised by the boss, and the new behaviour, such as asking for specific feedback, has not been fully adopted. Perhaps the coachee tried the new behaviour but without full conviction and it 'did not work'. The state of 'being in-between' can be very unsettling and the mantra, 'you have to let go in order to take hold', may not have been sufficiently convincing. The coachee's frustration, perhaps with herself, may be re-directed against the coach. Under these circumstances the coach will want to draw on the skills of 'support and challenge'. This means offering encouragement and praise, re-affirming the goal, helping the coachee practise the specific behaviours needed, visualising success and identifying additional sources of support. Above all, the coach should not panic!

Little has been achieved. The coachee's doubts may, on the other hand, not be part of a natural learning progress, but be a reflection of the reality that little has been achieved. If there have been regular reviews of progress this may not be a shock to the coach, but it can still happen. For example, the coachee may have been masking her dissatisfaction because she likes the coach, or is fearful of upsetting him, or has colleagues who say how great the coach has been for them. The task for the coach, having gathered more information from the coachee, is to take a long look at himself without self-blame and to consider, perhaps with the help of a peer or coaching supervisor, such questions as – *'have I generally been effective as a coach with my other coachees?', 'have I got into an unhelpful pattern with this particular coachee, and possibly done too much of the work?', 'have I kept the 'contract' under regular review?'.* There is then the possibility of moving forward – perhaps renegotiating the coaching agreement, or gathering more information on other factors which might be affecting the coachee's performance.

The coach's doubts. The coach might have doubts about the effectiveness of the coaching, even whilst the coachee is perfectly happy. There might be several causes; the coach has unrealistically high standards; the coachee is well behaved and acts from compliance rather than commitment; the coach is allowing 'outside' factors (for example 'difficulties' elsewhere, perhaps with other coachees) to cloud his judgement about what is, in fact, a highly productive coaching relationship. As in the earlier instances above, there is the need to gather some more information; for example the coach might need to ask the coachee, *'is there any way, however small, that you are dissatisfied with our work?, if you were unhappy about our work what would it be about?'.* The coach might also reflect on previous experiences of feeling this way and whether there was a theme; for example, whether it happened towards the end of a coaching relationship, when he was being reluctant to say good-bye to coachees he particularly liked. A rough rule of thumb for the coach in this is, at the beginning at least, to approach it all with a lightness of curiosity, avoiding burdening the coachee with his doubts.

Do we need other specialist help?

An analogy related to journeys could be the use of a river pilot for navigating a treacherous stretch of water. There may be occasions when the coach does not have the particular expertise, which the coachee needs. This might arise in a fairly low-key way; the coach has been brought in to help the coachee be more successful in handling promotion interviews; the pair makes good progress in terms of identifying past achievements and relating them to the anticipated demands of the new role. However the coach and the coachee, possibly in consultation with the sponsor, decide that some specialist help in self-presentation might be needed. So a specialist is brought in for a one-off session to help with voice modulation, movement and dress.

In contrast, the use of a specialist might be rather more demanding for all those involved. For example, it might have emerged early on in the coaching that the coachee has had some difficult childhood experiences. Both parties acknowledged this and had been very careful to work around them. The coachee might well have been able to make progress on some important job performance issues, but then 'hit a brick wall'. Dealing with the pain of the past became more urgent and increasingly important. There might then be discussions leading to an agreement that the coaching would cease whilst the coachee went to a therapist. Equally, the coaching might continue, but with a clear understanding that the existing boundaries would remain.

Coaches can become rather possessive of their coachees and then delude themselves that they can help with any need that may emerge. Sometimes coachees, inside or outside their awareness, support and foster a shared delusion. Perhaps it taps into a deep primal need that many of us might have, that there is one person who, like an all powerful mother or father, can make the world safe for us? The risk is that the coach becomes at best unhelpful and, at worst, behaves unethically. Negotiating and assisting a transition, temporary or permanent, to another helper is part of the coach's obligation. Only by holding the coachee with an open hand can the coach be truly supportive.

This is an interesting detour, but are we on the right road?

Since coaching is, by definition, about learning, there is always the possibility of the unexpected; perhaps indeed, promoting learning is about fostering the conditions where the unexpected is more likely? So on the coaching journey unexpected paths may appear, ones that were not on the original map. Their relevance or otherwise may not be immediately apparent. So we would urge the need for flexibility in these situations. One decision might be that the path is clearly leading directly away from Worthing and it makes no sense to follow it at this time; another decision might be to follow it for a while and see what emerges. Maybe it will turn out to be a quicker route to Worthing or will lead to the possibility of an even better destination?

In the midst of these options we would emphasise two points. First, the importance of some conscious decision-making, *'do we think this is likely to be helpful?, is it possibly so much of a diversion that we need to involve the sponsor because it may risk going beyond the original contract?, is this within my area of competence as a coach?, are we likely to breach the ethical framework?'.* Secondly, the coachee, and indeed the coach, may well feel some unease about this new path simply because of the fear and excitement which can accompany such choice-points. It may be important to 'sit' with those feelings for a while rather than rushing forwards or away. It is usually possible to continue down the original path and focus on, 'business as usual' for several sessions, then go back and explore the new route.

Have we really arrived?

There are several aspects to this. On occasions it may be a self-evident fact that what was sought has been achieved. Using the earlier example, the coachee has achieved the goal and passed the promotion interview.

It may be that the coach and coachee have reached the end of their relationship. It has a natural ending because there is nothing more the coach can offer or because the number of agreed sessions has been completed. In our experience it is surprising how often these two aspects converge, that the early establishment of a timescale gives a flow to the work that means it is automatically completed in the time available. Of course, this is not always the case. We have found it valuable to raise the question of possible ending before the last session (typically session four of a contracted six), so that it is clear whether it will take place at the time originally agreed. Sometimes another six sessions are contracted and another review held during the tenth session. We suggest this is an important way of avoiding rushed good-byes. Reflecting on the journey as a whole can consolidate learning and provide both coach and coachee with a clear basis for moving forward separately.

Doubts about whether the destination has been reached are sometimes fuelled by a desire not to say good-bye. The coach has a particular responsibility for ensuring clarity on this point. He may need to ask *'is there genuinely more work to be done? if so, am I the right person?'*. There may be a need to bring in a third party, for example the coachee's line manager, to help resolve these points.

In this chapter, we have sought to map out the territory of coaching in organisations. We have defined terms, considered some different coaching formats, described the broad phases of the coaching relationship, and identified the topics which might be covered in coaching. Finally, we have begun to consider some of the difficult issues that might arise. However, as is commonly said, 'the map is not the territory' and we wanted to include some quite personal material reflecting the real highs, lows, tensions and insights, which can arise for both coach and coachee. This is the content of the next chapter.

> *Taking care of a client*
> *does not*
> *inevitably mean*
> *disempowering him*

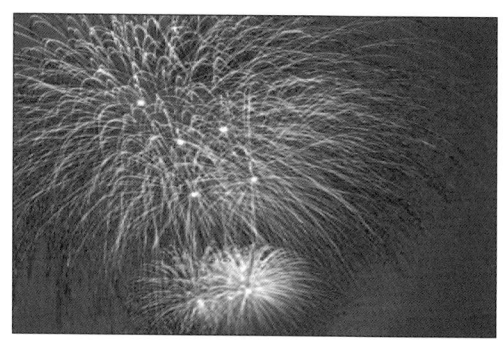

chapter three

Stories

What follows is a series of stories* illustrating the delights, difficulties and dilemmas of coaching. Sometimes there is a commentary further to elaborate the significance of the event. Some details have been changed to maintain confidentiality.

Our intention in writing this chapter is to ensure we bring the coaching process alive. We have, therefore, included sessions which did not run smoothly, or were not an unqualified success. No amount of theory and generalisation can adequately illustrate those fine points of judgement about going deeper, pulling back, offering suggestions, staying quiet, seeking to clarify or allowing the coachee to struggle with his confusion. With these stories we also wanted to emphasise that the coach is human too. She is not a totally detached and analytical observer; her feelings, perspectives, frailties and prejudices are an inevitable part of the process along with her insight, creativity and clear headedness.

The first section called 'coach on the couch' consists of personal recollections by coaches. Each story is a landmark for the coach for whom life was never quite the same afterwards. The experience, whether 'positive' or 'negative' led to some important learning. The second section, called 'the coachee speaks', is a series of equally personal recollections. We should also draw the reader's attention to appendix three which has some suggested guidelines for coachees. In our view, emphasis on the rights and responsibilities of the coachee is often neglected.

COACH ON THE COUCH

Becoming Mr Spock

I was coaching a client who was at a career crossroads. At the start of this one-off session

---

Please note that most of the storytellers generally used the word 'client' rather than 'coachee' when describing their experiences.

he was more aware of what he did not want from work, rather that what he did want. As our discussion progressed he made a passing reference to his hobby, mountaineering and said that he had vague thoughts about a possible new career abroad as a mountain guide. In exploring this with him he said that his major concern was making sure he saw enough of his young daughter (he was separated); he talked more about this, and said he would be very upset if he followed a new career and lost touch with her. In the midst of all this I suddenly began remembering my own elder daughter who was eight when my wife and I separated; subsequently I saw little of my daughter for several years.

As a coach I felt that it was important that none of my personal history should intrude into the session, especially since time was limited (a one-off session of two hours). Even though I was having some vivid memories I 'took myself in hand' and re-focused on the client. I took him through what I thought was a quite creative process where he imagined that his route to a new career was rather like a mountain path - vertiginous drops, shale, beautiful views - drawing analogies between this imagery and his reality. At the end of the session I felt that we had made good progress even though there were still many unanswered questions. The client thought it had been 'of some use'. However, in a later review it emerged that he felt it had largely been a waste of time, with my doing things for which he could not really see the purpose.

I was rather shocked, because after all had I not worked so hard to be helpful? However, I could not dismiss the client's feedback as uneducated ingratitude (much as I wanted to!). After some mature reflection, when I had stopped feeling like a sulky schoolboy, I realised the following; that when I thought I was being professional in pushing down my own feelings, I was actually being unhelpful to the client. In trying to get my own feelings under control and 'getting on with the job', I was trying to control the client, and pressurising him, however subtly, to take part in an exercise about which he had reservations. I did not slow down enough really to check with him what we were doing, other than to ask *'are you OK with this?'*. Essentially I had become Mr Spock, all thinking, no feeling and on automatic pilot.

My learning is that I really limited my options, believing that either I said nothing about the history with my daughter, or I had to give him the full story, the latter obviously being unfair and inappropriate. A better choice, for me and the client, would have been to mention very briefly what was happening to me and perhaps suggest a ten minute break.

A new director

I was asked to coach a newly appointed senior director of a manufacturing company. She had a technical background and had grown up in the company, but was nervous about her new role. We spent some time discussing what being a director meant and how it differed from an operational role. I sent her articles about the role of director and we discussed the skills required. We focused on the need for her to influence rather than 'tell', to take an overview rather than deal with all the operational detail and to build relationships outside the organisation to a much greater degree. We also discussed the whole issue of strategy development; what did it really mean and how do you do it? We got into quite a lot of detail about the strategic plan for her area and I acted as a sounding board for her thinking and sometimes suggested other ideas. I also offered suggestions as to how to express the ideas in a way that might fit the style of the Board and so get a good response.

After the focus on the strategic plan, the issues came around to her difficulty with one of her colleagues on the Board, who had been there a long time and, she felt, did not take her seriously. We explored how to work with and around this person and also how to gain the confidence of the managing director. I gave her some articles on politics in organisations, and on how to build personal power and we practised, in role play, ways of influencing.

After a couple of months, the focus turned to the impact on her home life of this new role. She was clear she wanted to meet the challenge and was primarily enjoying her wider responsibilities; we discussed some of the practical issues about making her life easier at home and about communicating with her husband about the inevitable impact on him.

We had ten sessions in all over a six month period and I believe she felt much more confident and settled as a result. The crucial aspect in it being successful seemed to have been my flexibility around the issues we covered and my not getting too fixed on why I was there (I had originally been chosen because of my strategy background). For example, I was able to switch into skill issues around influencing and politics.

The work-life balance discussion was heartfelt for me, as well as for her, and I had to judge how much of my own struggle with this to share with her. I find in areas that are topical for me, I am most likely to move into giving too much advice and talking too much! I found it useful to check out my approach around this topic with my supervisor and fellow coach.

Staying grown up

I was coaching a strong-minded senior manager who had been rapidly promoted in a niche IT company. At one stage in the coaching she spoke of the private pangs of doubt she experienced from time-to-time, and that when she did she felt like a young girl. I asked her what age she felt at those times and she said fourteen. I said that if she wished we could explore this a little further, but that we would both need to be very careful about going too far into the past, and opening up issues which were more appropriate to counselling than coaching; she agreed. I then asked her what attitudes she felt she brought to work when she felt like a fourteen year old. She replied 'lacking in confidence, rebellious and creative'. The session then continued with our considering each of these aspects, whether and how they helped or hindered her in her job, and the actions she might take.

Alerting the client to the potential risks of a particular line of enquiry can be a fine point of judgement. Here I was helped enormously by the fact that this was my third session with her. We had developed quite a lot of trust and there were more sessions planned. She had also read a lot about training and therapy, so we could both recognise the significance of the decision point and treat it as fellow professionals. On other occasions with other clients it has been more difficult, because in explaining the choice point I have evoked anxiety in the client. Then, in offering an explanation, intended to be reassuring, I have generated even more unease. Of course it might well have been I who was anxious and inadvertently transmitting my feelings to the coachee.

From this arises the question, of what is really meant by the word equality in the coaching relationship? There should obviously be equality in terms of mutual respect and the potential for both parties to learn. However, the coach is there to help the client; if it also happens the other way round then it is either a happy bonus or possibly a total distortion of the basis of the relationship. It can sometimes be unhelpful to explain the choice point in the coaching process because the client has enough to handle in terms of the content.

Reflecting back on that earlier coaching session with the female manager, I can find another reason why my decision to alert her to the dangers of our getting into counselling issues was right. She had fought against a fair degree of sexism, albeit subtle, in her career. As a male coach, my pushing her in a direction with which she was not comfortable might have, understandably, provoked her to a lot of resistance.

For me the most important learning was the recognition that taking care of the client does not necessarily mean that I disempower her. Subsequently, I had quite a few clients who had much less experience of coaching and personal development. I became much more measured in the amount of information I gave them about the process and was simpler and clearer in the choices I offered them in how we might work together.

Whose needs?

My client was a well-established specialist in recruitment and selection for a large company in the financial services sector. He had asked me to become his coach because he felt he was not coping well in managing his newly dispersed team.

For the first couple of sessions I felt that we were working well together and so did he. We seemed to be 'on the same wavelength'. We analysed his change of responsibilities and the new challenges he faced. We had a great time teasing apart the true definition of words. We discussed, for example, what 'an acceptable level of performance' really means.

It was with some confidence that I took an audiotape of one of these sessions to my coaching supervisor. I was anticipating good marks on 'developing rapport'! She commented on how excited we sounded on the tape in our forensic examination of the meaning of words; she then said that it sounded rather 'intellectual' and asked if I felt I was making progress with the client. In the discussion that followed I realised that I had done very little to explore the client's feelings. In fact I was treating the client too much like a professional colleague; my needs were being met, but perhaps not his.

So, in taking a new tack with the coachee at the next session, I began to uncover the extent to which he felt the loss of daily contact with his team. We had both been working at the level of problem-solving when actually there were more immediate issues of loss and grief to be considered. So I had actually been hindering him, and he had allowed me, but neither of us had realised this.

What I took from this experience was the importance of stepping back from the coaching and really challenging myself about the value of a session, even if it has apparently gone well.

Calling a halt

I coached a senior executive over several months. We met every three weeks for a two-hour session; we met offsite so she would not be bothered by interruptions.

The presenting issue was her relationship with her boss. She felt he did not listen and was not always honest with her. I took a risk and asked her about her father. She recognised there was a similarity between her boss's behaviour and his. We were then able to discuss how difficult that made it to be assertive with her boss and to find the right way of influencing him. We worked on ways of dealing with him both in general terms and specifically. Sometimes we would unpick specific incidents that had happened to see how she could have handled things differently. At other times we would talk about events coming up, such as a joint presentation or her appraisal, where we thought about how to prepare for it. Some of the process focused on behaviour, some on her attitude and the possibility that she was over-reacting due to the fact that she 'saw her father in him'. This went fine but I felt nervous all the time in trying not to stray too far into the counselling arena. How far is too far remained on my mind and I talked it through with my supervisor many times.

After several sessions, she spoke a little about her husband and the fact that all was not well; then one day she confided in me that she was thinking of leaving him; she wanted to talk it through and we did. Over the next few sessions, the issue of her relationship with her husband started to dominate the sessions; other confidences came out. I began to feel that I really had strayed into a counselling role and that some of the issues raised required a deeper look at her life and past than was appropriate in a coaching setting. I was also beginning to feel that I ran the risk of acting as a confessor. Some of what we covered did not fit well with my own values. I kept coming away from the sessions feeling anxious that somehow I was doing the wrong thing, although the client seemed grateful and comfortable.

I took my confusion to my supervisor and we concluded that my client really needed to seek a different sort of support for this issue and that maybe we should begin to plan the end of our sessions, particularly as her relationship with her boss was much improved. It was quite a tricky issue to raise; how to do it in a way that was supportive to her but also did not compromise my own values? In fact, I ducked the issue of my 'judgement' of her; I merely stuck to the fact we were starting to look at personal issues predominantly and that this was not appropriate. She agreed we should end and we had two finishing sessions and left it there. We lost contact and I have always wondered how the story ended and whether my unwillingness to continue as a confessor was eventually a useful confrontation for her. My learning was to recognise how easily I could, as a coach, slip into the role of confidante. It was only the fact that I had a supervisor that made me face up to this. Whether I handled the ending well I am not altogether sure.

Magic moments

It is fairly common in both sport and management to refer to 'peak performance'...... the moment when all the skills come together, seamlessly, with an intensity of concentration, which is, paradoxically, effortless. In coaching this means a rhythm with the client where we both dance to the same tune and are 'in the flow'. A recent example for me was a case when I allowed myself to give full attention to the client, putting aside all 'shoulds'. In using my intuition, honesty and transparency with this particular client, she began to sparkle and even as I looked at her she grew younger, recounting her achievement of the goals we had agreed. She had transformed herself and I had the privilege of being a witness.

Of course I know not all coaching is like this; sometimes I dance with the client, but it is to different rhythms, or we are in different rooms, or it feels as if the client is in the corridor having a cigarette! Yet a magic moment, such as that described above, is something I treasure without making it the burden of a yardstick by which I judge my work. To insist on a magic moment each session or even each day would be unbearable for me, let alone the client.

Avoiding Abilene

Early in my career I came across the Abilene Paradox[1] in William G. Dyer's book[2] on team building. It was one of those moments when something goes 'kerrching!' in the dark recesses of the mind and you know that the sentiments of the tale will stay embedded forever. Briefly, and with apologies to the author, it is a story of a group of people ending up where none of them wanted to be because no-one had dared to object, because everyone else seemed to want to fall in with the plan.

---

[1] *J Harvey 'Managing Agreement in Organisations: The Abilene Paradox' published in Organisational Dynamics, Summer 1974.*
[2] *W G Dyer 'Team Building – Issues and Actions'. Addison – Wesley*

Many years later I was strongly reminded of the story on one of my coaching assignments.

I recall working in the UK Division of one particular organisation with a strong European parent. The UK Division was going through the all-too-familiar reorganisation and even had the help of a prestigious firm of worldwide consultants! I had been retained to do some coaching work with the directors and senior managers of its customer service operation. This followed a large-scale change programme my consultancy had successfully completed in that division.

The general idea of the re-organisation was the familiar one of producing a more customer-facing structure and a set of systems designed to give a competitive edge and a better bottom line.

Against this background coaching commenced. After a while the first executive began to report his fears about the 'new order'. Essentially the reorganisation seemed like a paper exercise to give new titles to the top level and everything else was to be renamed but nothing substantial seemed to be changing. Scant regard was being paid to what customers wanted. The worldwide consultants seemed to be rolling out their own versions of what should be done in a manner that was at odds with the culture supposedly being created alongside the new structures. The local senior management team felt they were being sidelined by the chief executive.

One by one, the coachees reported similar stories to me as if each was the only one to have seen the problem.

Oh dear! The whole organisation seemed to be going on a trip to Abilene and no one was speaking up! So these very able and intelligent people were feeling the stress and pressure that comes with these situations. Clearly there were issues of behaviour for all of them as well. For example, how to introduce the concerns into the main project meeting or weekly executive meeting without being labelled negative and incurring the wrath of the 'boss'?

There were so many issues presenting in those early coaching meetings that I might have become overwhelmed. However, I kept reminding myself that coaches are not messiahs or organisational saviours and whilst all potential aspects were fascinating I had to concentrate on helping each individual find his or her route through and avoid trying to influence the organisation by proxy. So, for the directors, our sessions concentrated on ways of clearly working out winning strategies and tactics for the organisation and the behaviours necessary to work effectively and assertively as members of the 'top team'. For the senior managers we concentrated on behaviours to help bring power to their own roles and relationships, vertical and horizontal; for one or two individuals it was about how to disengage from the organisation in a positive way and begin a new and different, fulfilling career. In all of this, absolute confidentiality was maintained and if issues arose that could not be 'held' we found ways for the individual to raise it within the organisation.

I also made sure we never finished a session without having some clear actions to achieve by the next session. The first steps did not have to be earth shattering; often we would agree a rehearsal in circumstances that were more comfortable for the individual before agreeing to do it for real in the boss's arena. Many of our sessions were high energy and spent standing at the flip chart with a pen, each using our skill and knowledge to grind out an understanding, a solution or set of actions. The sessions were never cosy chats; they were hard work.

Also, I had to be uncharacteristically organised to follow through at the beginning of each subsequent session and be demanding if no attempts at the agreed action had been taken. I think some people call this a 'tough love' approach. To their great credit all the individuals involved battled through their discomfort and emerged as seasoned independent travellers.

What all these people seemed to be after was a feeling of belonging and some help in working out the means to achieve the interventions that they knew were necessary. Slowly but surely small successes were reported that grew into a much wider sense of the organisation really getting to grips with the issues that had always been around but that no amount of neatly drawn organisation charts could put right. They were no longer going to Abilene!

The organisation is still changing, but people seem more comfortable that it is going in the right direction and are no longer so afraid to speak up. I hope they keep up their good work. I think the worldwide consultants were last seen on the outskirts of Abilene looking for a new client!

THE COACHEE SPEAKS

From the following stories it can be seen that the relevance and impact of the coaching is obviously variable and highly personal. However, if we were, on behalf of the coachee, to emphasise one point, it would be the importance of being assertive with the coach, and not getting into a patient-doctor mind-set, assuming that she must know best.

The virtue of promiscuity

An important part of my development as a client has been to draw consciously on a variety of coaches. Whilst having one coach to whom I regularly turn, there are others in a loose network with whom I have one-off sessions. In particular I have learnt the value of going to people who seem to have a quite different approach to life; sometimes it has been difficult, but almost always enlightening. For example, I have been looking for ways to change the basis of my consultancy, to pursue my interest in sailing, and to combine this with management development, specifically outward bound. As a way of pursuing this I decided to re-write my promotional literature, and get some feedback. My 'main coach', whilst praising my willingness to take risks, encouraged me to take some tests to re-assess my core competencies. He also recommended another coach with whom I had a one-off session, taking me back to some absolute fundamentals about the business sector at which I was aiming, and whether I wanted to market myself directly to customers or through other consultancies. I got valuable new perspectives from both these people, but as important was the process I went through in accepting their criticisms and suggestions as worthy of consideration, fighting my own temptation to argue with them, trying to prove them wrong. I wanted to scream at them, *'can't you see I'm trying to do something which is new and exciting for me! All you're offering me is dead-pan logic and little obvious encouragement!'*. So I have learnt the value of getting coaching from people with whom I may not feel totally comfortable.

Little things can mean a lot

I once had a coach who did not allow himself a break between sessions. Surprisingly he seemed to be able to tune into me very quickly and easily. He, for example, never called me by the name of his previous client! However, the room always had the smell of the previous occupant (not unpleasant, but certainly distinctive) and somehow their feelings were still in the air. We were just contracted to have six sessions at monthly intervals, and I kept making the excuse to myself that it was a petty matter not worth raising. However, I wish I had said something because I used to lose the first ten minutes of each session dealing with my reactions; but perhaps an aerosol spray would have been worse!

I began talking about a customer who had made me really angry. I could hear myself getting louder. The coach got up and shut the window, with no word of explanation or apology. I can see now that he was worried about confidentiality, but the impact on me was as if I had been told to be quiet and shut up.

I was asked by my coach to use my imagination to envisage some new career goals. This was in some ways a reasonable request, but very difficult in a small, cramped, windowless office.

Keeping clear

We were three coachees and the coach. One of the other coachees was resistant to the methods that the coach was using about visualising what it would be like to take a certain course of action. This coachee also took up a disproportionate amount of the group's time by blocking suggested techniques and being indecisive. After several sessions we, the coachees, had exchanged e-mails and phone numbers. I was phoned by one of the coachees and told that she liked the way I approached problems better than did the coach. I responded by saying that I was not her coach and that she should talk to the coach about this. The subject never came up again between us. I did not say anything to the coach as I felt it was the other coachee's responsibility to bring up her own issues; but I was also motivated by the fact that I did not want to hurt the coach either. I think that I protected my own integrity but could I have done anything differently to facilitate the other's relationship?

At the simplest level my learning point is that if I have responsibility as coach for a group I will try to make roles and responsibilities clear and emphasise what people should do if they are not happy with the coaching session.

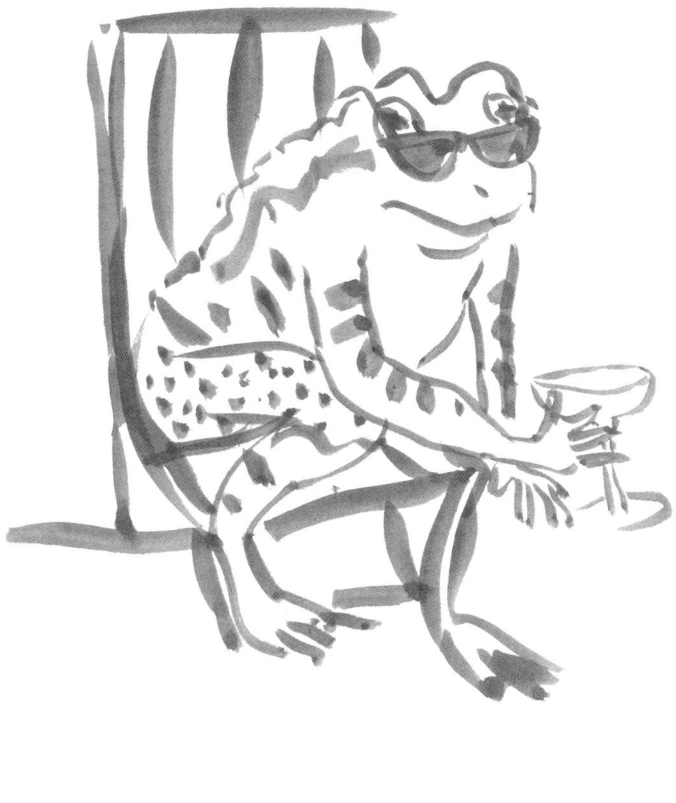

The frog in a deckchair

I am at session three of a coaching series. What I wanted to try and sort out was what new direction in my work life I wanted to take. I was faced with a couple of options and was finding it hard to decide.

In the first session, I talked about these two options as you might expect. Much to my surprise, the coach pointed out to me that when I talked about what I **should** do, I slumped back in my chair and looked down and when I talked about what I **wanted** to do I leant forward and became more animated. He suggested I adopted the second bodily posture and told him again about the options. Strange as it sounds in adopting the 'want to' bodily position I felt a lot clearer about what I wanted. The truth is that what I want at present is to take a less stressful option, but I am used to pushing myself to do the best I can, going for the more career-based option; that is, I tend to do what I feel I should. The exercise helped me to be clearer about what I wanted – if only I give myself permission.

In the second session, we built on this further. The coach listened to my rather analytical approach to what I might do next, but then asked me to imagine different parts of me that might have differing views. One image that came out loud and clear was that of a frog, in sunglasses, with a glass of red wine, sitting by a swimming pool on holiday. Again this, for me, rather an unusual way of working, helped me to realise the degree to which I wanted to let myself off the hook and find a better work-life balance, to use a rather hackneyed phrase. If we had just problem-solved and goal-set around what I thought I wanted, which was choosing between two career options, I do not think I would have realised the strength of feeling I had around not really wanting either option. The problem-solving part of the session then continued with whether it was possible to take time off or work part-time; in other words, to have what I really wanted.

The third session took a different turn. I felt very muddled about a work incident with a colleague that had gone badly wrong; I felt unclear as to whether I expect too much of others or whether I was being unfairly treated. The coach gave me a very clear view; he had heard some of the ongoing saga. He said that in his view I was being badly treated and that I kept trying to make something work whereas the other party did not seem to be making a similar effort. He also said, *'I do not think you have anything more to learn from this situation and you should walk away'*.

I felt quite gob-smacked at the vehemence of his view. It was uncharacteristic of him. I also felt relieved and, at an instinctive level, I felt he was right. I did not feel pushed into a course of action but I was grateful for a strong opinion. Sometimes, the 'what do you think?' approach can be quite frustrating. After musing some more, talking to others and living with the idea for a while, I did in fact act on the coach's advice. And I still feel it was the right thing to do.

We included this section on stories to emphasise that theories and models can only approximate reality. We imagine, for example, that many a coach has, like us, suddenly thought in the middle of a session, *'how do I handle this? Nothing in my text books warned me this might happen!'*. We take this theme further in the next chapter where we consider some of the mistakes coaches can make and ways of avoiding or dealing with them.

> *If coaches have a background in training then they may carry with them not only finely-honed listening skills but a lingering addiction to the smell of greasepaint*

Stories

chapter four

Some common pitfalls

There can of course be many reasons why a coaching session, or series of sessions, is less successful. In this chapter we concentrate on describing those which, in our experience, are less readily recognised. The ultimate impact of these pitfalls can vary extensively. A relatively minor example might be where a coach 'shows off' and wastes ten minutes by presenting the coachee with unnecessary and unwanted theory. At the other extreme, the whole basis of the relationship might be undermined because the coach colludes with the coachee in approaching her as if she were a wayward child.

COLLUSION WITH THE COACHEE

First, a word of explanation about what we mean by the word 'collusion'. In its more everyday use it means a secret agreement, often for an illegal purpose. With this definition, for example, a bank official and his customer might collude to defraud the bank. This is not how we use the word when referring to problems in the coaching relationship. The crucial difference is 'awareness'. In coaching, when referring to collusion, we are not talking about a conscious conspiracy. Rather, we are describing the unhelpful meshing of unaware patterns of behaviour between the coach and coachee. Much has been written about it in books on therapy and counselling[3].

Collusion is not a consciously-contrived ritual, but one that is played out on 'automatic pilot'. Sometimes the collusive process would be obvious to the disinterested bystander; the coachee enters the room crestfallen and pathetic saying, *'I am afraid I messed up again'*. The coach in response oozes love, support and sympathy spending the next hour trying to make the coachee feel better. When the coachee finally leaves the room, probably at least ten minutes late, then the coach feels frustrated and exhausted because of doing too much of

---

[3] *One of the best illustrations is Steve Karpman's 'Drama Triangle'. See 'Transactional Analysis After Eric Berne'. Graham Barnes (Ed.) Harpers College Press.*

the work. Collusion will often not be as 'technicolour' as this. The following 'coach on the couch' story presents a more monochrome version.

'The coachee entered the room flustered saying he was upset because he had just heard that he, along with his team, was going to have to move to cheaper offices because of a drop in business. I spent the session identifying possible actions with him. On reflection I realised that I never quite pinned him down to specific actions. Not only that, I did not follow up on the commitments he had made the previous session. I had become so caught up with his feeling bad, that I held back from challenging him enough. In the stress of the situation he became too woolly and I became too 'soft'.'

Some aspects of these unaware patterns may be more easily surfaced than others. As mentioned elsewhere, professional development, supervision and peer feedback can all help the coach become more aware of any unhelpful habits she might have. However, we want to emphasise here the contribution that one aspect of coaching best practice can make; that of note-taking. We imagine that most coaches will make notes of the content of their coaching sessions. We further suggest that in addition to these 'content' notes the coach also captures some rather more speculative issues. These could cover the coach's feelings. Did she come away from the session pleased, confused, uneasy? Did she have any very strong feelings about any particular comment or behaviour from the coachee? Were there aspects of the coachee's behaviour she found difficult to handle? Were there any interventions the coach was particularly pleased with?

The value of these notes is not only related to working with that one coachee. Notes from work with several coachees can also be reviewed over time, considering any themes or patterns that might arise. There can be some valuable learning about types of coachee or issue. For example, the coach might realise that she is particularly effective in working with ambitious, senior, male managers, by being clear, simple, direct and challenging. However, on reflection, she realises that she can be a little over-protective with junior staff. This awareness then brings the coach choices about how she might then enhance her skills. She might, with help, want to explore the underlying dynamic. This might lead to the recognition that in her childhood she spent a lot of time looking after her younger sister, and that she has brought a little too much of that attitude into her current working with junior staff. Equally, the coach might decide not to explore her personal history, but focus specifically on identifying how she is effective with senior managers, and then applying consciously those skills with junior staff.

We return to this fundamental topic of collusion on several more occasions in this book.

OVER-RELIANCE ON OBJECTIVES

Some readers may be surprised, even appalled to see this sub-heading. They might ask, *'how can you assess your progress if you do not know where you want to go?'*. We are simply questioning a basic assumption - that objectives are by definition a 'good thing' and that coaches should always be helping their coachees to establish them.

There are many frameworks for the coaching process and most of them involve the early setting of objectives with the coachee. This then becomes the reference point for the later stages; we try to clarify the support needed, assess progress, identify next steps and then review the current validity of the objectives. Often, this may be totally appropriate, perhaps, particularly, where the coaching is focused on skills.

Our reservations centre around three main areas. First, sometimes the question faced by the coachee is *'if I do not know who I am, how can I know what I want?'*. In stating it so boldly we suggest that coachees - and not necessarily just those facing an existential crisis - sometimes need time to go exploring, having the freedom to follow their curiosity, being open to the possibilities that may then present themselves. For example, a coachee might be interested in a possible job change. In response, the coach might agree with him a number of objectives; visiting specific individuals, reading certain books, getting information from the web. In doing this, the coach and coachee may narrow the focus too quickly and, paradoxically, make it too purposeful. An alternative, which might be more appropriate at times, would be for the coachee simply to pay attention to what he notices during the following week (at work, home, watching television, gardening) and what really takes his interest. From that may come totally unexpected clues about careers, and indeed many other matters.

Our second reservation is that in some organisations objectives sustain a fantasy world where they are chosen simply on the basis that they can be measured, rather than having any inherent relevance. It reminds us of the story about the drunk who only looks for his lost keys under the lamp post because that is the only place with any light. So the drive to establish objectives in coaching can mark a process of collusion with the existing organisational culture. Perhaps anyway, the coachee's performance is not as strong as it might be because of working in an organisation where objectives are not taken seriously, or where they are imposed, or both.

Thirdly, the push for objectives can say more about the coach's insecurities than the coachee's real needs. The coach feels under pressure to prove his worth, translating this proof into the requirement that the coachee should always leave the session with some specific objectives. There can be a strand of insanity in this; following the coaching framework becomes more important than following the coachee's process; the coach can only see himself as effective if the coachee 'performs', that is, does what the coach expects of him. A rather unhealthy mutual emotional dependency might ensue which can disempower both parties.

LACK OF VARIETY IN APPROACH

Understandably coaches have their own styles and as part of this each will have his favourite tools and techniques. Our concern is simply where these habits end up having a life of their own regardless of the client need. We might believe, for example, that if it is session two we should be using 360-degree feedback. This may be appropriate, but equally, it may not. Supervision, peer review, and continuous professional development can all help ensure an appropriate variety of technique. We consider this point again later when looking at situations where coaches work in teams; we must remember they can, at worst, reinforce each other's regimented paucity of approach.

PERFORMING/TRYING TO LOOK CLEVER

This is about coaches meeting their own needs rather than the coachee's. Coaches have an interesting and exciting range of tools at their disposal. Some are described in appendix four. When coachees are 'stuck' and even when they are not, it can be a temptation to 'pull something out of the hat', the motivation being to show off. There was an element of that in 'Becoming Mr Spock' in chapter three. Coachees who are eager, sometimes desperate, for help can be overly susceptible to the coach 'making a suggestion'. If coaches have a background in training then they may carry with them not only finely honed listening skills, but also a lingering addiction to the smell of greasepaint….

OVER INVESTMENT IN THE COACHEE MAKING CHANGES

There will nearly always be the coachee who affects us a little more deeply in some way.

We might be saddened by some of his life experience or filled with admiration at his courage and tenacity, or, heaven forbid, desperate for him to be humbled in some way. We would suggest that if ever the coach has a particularly strong reaction, 'positive' or 'negative' to a coachee, then it is good practice to ask oneself, *'why am I making this person so important to me?'*. Sometimes the discoveries will be totally acceptable and honourable. At other times there may be something happening that is not helping the overall coaching process.

*'I really want him to seize this new job opportunity...but perhaps it's more about **my** not feeling stretched enough in **my** work'; 'I really want the coachee to stand up to her boss more...but perhaps it's about **my** needing to be more assertive in **my** life'; 'I really want the coachee to take more risks...but perhaps it's more about **my** not having taken the risk of telling him how much I admire the progress he has made'; 'I really want the coachee to decide to finish the coaching relationship....but perhaps it's more about **my** fancying her and **my** struggling with **my** feelings'.*

Sometimes these realisations will be liberating; at other times they may also point to a journey of personal learning, perhaps one that the coach had assumed was already complete.

UNREALISTIC EXPECTATIONS OF SELF AND COACHEE

Particularly when coaching in the performance and life domains, one can believe that there have to be insightful breakthroughs at each session. We may even have fantasies, which occasionally become reality, of the coachee standing up and saying, *'I see EVERYTHING so differently now. THANK YOU'*. A more realistic expectation is that sometimes there will be sessions which will be really hard work; that there is solid, but unspectacular progress. Perhaps the insights will take place between sessions? It may even be that the coach does not get much credit at all because she did such a good job helping the coachee take responsibility.

Linked closely to this is the need to accept that there may well be loose ends at the end of a session and that the coachee may even feel confused. This can be a very healthy sign - that the coachee has relinquished certain unhelpful beliefs or behaviours, and he is simply not sure with what to replace them. Of course, it might just be that the coach has run a rubbish session!

Expectations need to be matched to the circumstances – time available, willingness of the client, and organisational support. Having realistic expectations requires the coach to pay attention to her own well-being. If the coach is exhausted (for example, by taking on too many clients, or not allowing sufficient breaks between sessions) then she will lose perspective and inevitably becoming less effective. She may fight too many battles, or move from genuine concern to clinical smiling, or seek comfort from the client. At their worst such behaviours can help create a painful, spiralling, vicious circle. We suggest, therefore, that having a good 'support network' (please excuse the jargon) is particularly vital for those, internal or external, who work largely on their own. Members of this network could range from professional peers, with whom the coach can examine the detail of their work, through to friends who know nothing about coaching and who hopefully wish to maintain this state of blissful ignorance!

FAILURE TO RE-CONTRACT

The concerns that the coachee brings to the early sessions may prove not to be the 'real' or most important issues. This may be because the coachee is wisely 'playing it safe' -going to Dorking (see chapter two). He brings a relatively 'minor' problem along until he can decide whether or not to trust the coach. An alternative scenario is that, with further exploration, perhaps taking several sessions, it becomes clear that the situation is different from what had been assumed. It may be, for example, that the coachee does not really want a new job, rather he wants to be more effective in handling his boss. This switch should be clearly identified and agreed; it might require some discussion about whether or how to go back to the sponsor of the coaching for example. The discovery of new information or insights may signal that the coach is moving outside her area of competence. This might mean the coachee needs counselling or therapy, or needs to switch to a coach who has the relevant skills in, say, business strategy. It can be tempting to let things drift, or to 'do one's best' to meet the need; this is unlikely to prove a wise decision.

When considering such pitfalls, as we have described above, it is difficult to overestimate the value of having a coaching supervisor. In counselling and therapy the role of the supervisor is well understood. Essentially this person oversees the work of the counsellor or therapist, being available to deal with a variety of concerns, for example, lack of progress, ethical issues, or possible collusion. Any contact the supervisor might possibly have with the client should be strictly limited, in our view. Coaching is still seeking to establish its professional territory, and supervision is often haphazard or non-existent. Whilst coaches wait for or contribute to professional standards they can also seek out those who might offer

Some common pitfalls

supervision. An experienced colleague or trusted contact from the many coaching networks, could be a good candidate for this role.

In this chapter we have drawn on our more difficult experiences to identify some of the common, but perhaps less easily recognised, ways in which coaches can reduce their effectiveness. A summarising rule of thumb we suggest from this is, 'treat turbulence and calm with equal caution'. In other words, just as turbulence can be a sign of things going right, rather than wrong, so calm can mean compliance rather that commitment.

We now move onto that part of the book devoted to looking at coaching through the eyes of various stakeholders. First, we start with the coach's manager…..

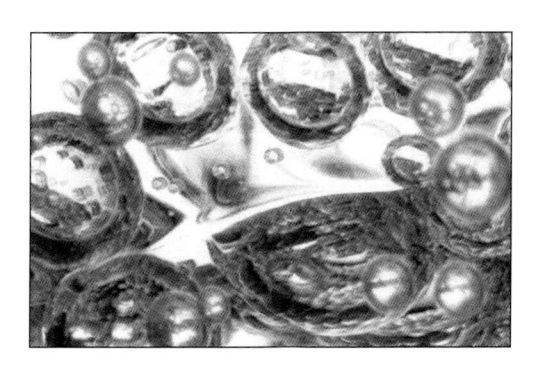

chapter five

Perspectives – the coach's manager

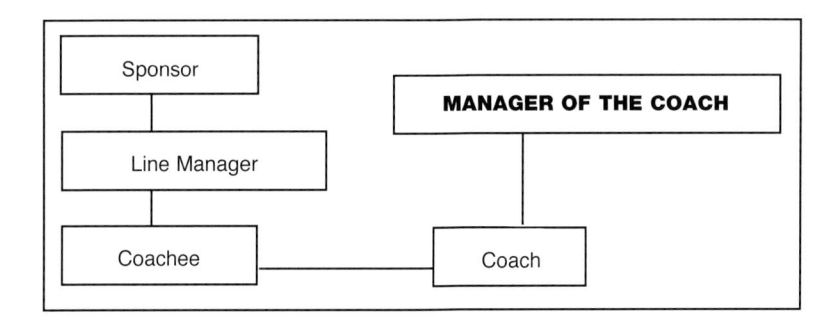

```
┌─────────────────────────────────────────────────┐
│   ┌─────────┐                                   │
│   │ Sponsor │        ┌──────────────────────┐   │
│   └────┬────┘        │ MANAGER OF THE COACH │   │
│        │             └──────────┬───────────┘   │
│   ┌────┴────────┐               │               │
│   │Line Manager │               │               │
│   └────┬────────┘               │               │
│        │                        │               │
│   ┌────┴────┐            ┌──────┴──┐            │
│   │ Coachee │────────────│  Coach  │            │
│   └─────────┘            └─────────┘            │
└─────────────────────────────────────────────────┘
```

It is all too easy to see coaching as solely a relationship between two people - the coach and coachee. However, both practically and emotionally, there will be other presences in the coaching room. In this chapter we consider the coach's manager. This can be a vital relationship, remembering that what the coach offers is partly dependent upon what he receives. So, for example, the coach may well be less able to offer his coachee support if he is not supported by his own manager. One could argue that the relationship between the coach and his manager has to be of a high quality – authentic, straightforward, mutually respectful and constructively challenging – as a necessary pre-condition for the coach to begin working with his coachee in a similar way. Below we describe how the coach's manager can begin to offer these qualities.

BALANCING INVOLVEMENT AND DETACHMENT

In the world of consultancy, the project director is a well-established role. This is the person who, for example, takes the strategic overview of a change management initiative, ensuring coherence between all the various components. For the external consultancy team it probably means a leader who deliberately avoids getting involved in operational detail. He is, for example, unlikely to take a significant role in actually delivering any workshops which might be part of the change strategy. When translated into the world of coaching there are some fine points of judgement.

The manager of coaches getting involved in the coaching? Such non-attachment is particularly important when translated into the role of manager of coaches; yet it is a boundary, which can easily, almost imperceptibly, dissolve. The manager of coaches can easily be seduced into becoming coach to the sponsors of change projects. When this happens a number of possible problems can arise.

First, there is a likely conflict of interest. The manager of coaches, whilst supporting the coachee, will probably want to sell more business. When considering the question, *'what is my investment in this person and client?'* – as all coaches need to - then the possibility of a reasonably objective view is, we would suggest, almost impossible when some strong commercial agendas are at stake.

Secondly, difficulties might arise impeding effective coaching supervision. If the manager of coaches becomes coach to the sponsor, then he may well become privy to a lot of sensitive information - for example, relating to personnel issues, finances or the future restructuring of the business. All this would be automatically covered by a confidentiality agreement, as part of any normal coaching arrangement. This information, even though it cannot be revealed to them, may be of vital interest to other coaches also working in the organisation. So the manager of coaches may be in the invidious position that he is trying to help one of his coaches deal with an awkward coaching problem, but he cannot divulge information which could be very helpful.

Let us illustrate this with an example. The coach wants supervision on how to intervene with the coachee who is struggling to assert himself in a new role. The manager of coaches may know from the sponsor that this particular role is due to be phased out in a few months. The immediate, equally unattractive, choices are to breach confidentiality or engage in a charade.

Thirdly, by 'entering the fray' and taking on a coaching role in the client organisation, the manager of coaches denies himself the opportunity to be an honest broker; for example, he is less able to handle complaints about the coaching or mediate between managers. As mentioned before, it is impossible to know in advance what issues might arise, so the manager of coaches might start coaching, believing that there will be no conflict of interest, but then discover that there is. The disentangling could be quite awkward – *'what, if anything, to say to whom, and when'* – and need not have arisen in the first place.

Combining coaching and team building. This leads to another tricky area, when coaching and team-building are combined, a not an uncommon occurrence. If somebody has been a coach to one or more team members and then takes on the role of team builder to that team, it can become almost impossible to work effectively, let alone ethically. By definition many confidences are shared in coaching, and the coach, when acting as team builder, will probably find it impossible to remember which of those items are not in the 'public domain'. In seeking to help the team move forward - by possibly using a more directive style than typified the coaching – the team builder could easily 'let something slip'. She may realise it at the time, but to mention it may simply 'make it worse'. She may comment later to the relevant coachee and try to retrieve the situation. She may not realise it at all, but gradually become aware that suddenly her coachee, and other members of the team who may have noticed what happened, have somewhat distanced themselves from her.

As well as the dangers of 'letting something slip', coaches will often interpret their role as the creation of an alliance with the coachee; there will be something of a 'special relationship'. So in running a team event it would be difficult for the coach not to feel extra support for 'her' coachee, being less able to balance the needs of all the members of the team. Commonly, team events require the facilitator to take the role of mediator as differences of interest are worked through. In this potentially charged atmosphere the facilitator who also has some coaching relationships may well struggle to remain sufficiently objective. In our view, team-building and coaching are best done by separate consultants.

So, the coach's manager faces some interesting challenges in terms of being sufficiently involved to know enough about what is going on, but to stay sufficiently detached in order to see the issues and the people clearly. An important way of finding and maintaining the right balance is to give a high priority to the development of the coaching team. We now move onto this in more detail.

DEVELOPING COACHES AS INDIVIDUALS AND AS A TEAM

As is apparent from what we have already written, it is vital that the coach has others to turn to for ideas, insights, sanity checks, supervision and emotional support. If the coach is a member of a team then all this may be 'on tap', though not necessarily so. Either way, the manager of coaches has a role, indeed obligation, in ensuring that each coach is as well equipped as possible. We suggest, therefore, that attention is paid to:

Clear, ethical standards. The coach must contribute to these and agree a framework for working (see appendix five). Such standards are central to contracting with all the stakeholders. Of course, not every eventuality can be identified in advance, but often possible difficulties can be pre-empted. For example, the sponsor might expect to receive feedback on the 'performance' of the coachees, unless the issue of confidentiality is raised and understood from the very beginning.

Training and supervision. The coach brings examples of work on a regular basis for review. This may be based on clients or issues with which the coach is having difficulty, but might equally be about identifying and sharing why some coaching has been particularly successful. This may take place within the coaching team. If not, then clearly the learning has to be brought back and discussed with colleagues.

Continuing professional development. The coach updates his skills on a regular basis, and new thinking and new publications about coaching are reviewed and possibly used.

Workload. If the coach gets too tired then one of the first consequences is a loss of clarity about boundaries; they may become too fluid or too rigid. So the coach may, often without realising it, become almost totally absorbed into the coachee's perspective or conversely armoured against seeing the coachee's point of view. Either of these can happen quite subtly without either party realising. If left unattended, then the problems are likely to become more severe – illness, inappropriate challenging, persistent lateness, disrespect to the coachee and breaches of confidentiality. Also if the coach has a lot happening in his personal life, he may owe it to himself, his colleagues and his coachees to reduce his coaching workload significantly, or even stop for a while.

All of the above are highly relevant for the team as a whole. Additionally, there are other points that the manager of coaches and the team may well need to consider:

Agreeing a broad consistency of approach. This might cover style, techniques and focus for the work. We are not suggesting that each coach should work in exactly the same way; this would create its own tyranny. Rather we are recommending that the team should be alert to extremes. For example, the coach who always takes a strong skills focus whilst his colleague is always focusing on life issues. Putting aside the vital issue of client needs, there is the simple matter of product consistency. If the coachees were to compare notes and discuss it with the sponsor, is the difference of approach explicable and justifiable? All members of the coaching team and their manager need a good understanding of any differences of approach. The coach's manager in particular should be well equipped to handle the sponsor's questions or concerns.

Equally, with knowledge of each coach's aptitude and style, a better match can be made with the client's needs.

Being alert to the risks of collusion. We have already touched on the risks of collusion between individuals. This can also happen between groups, for example, the coaching team and the client organisation. Outside their awareness (sometimes even with awareness), organisations can invite in consultancies who help them stay stuck rather than move forward. For example, an organisation drowning in a sea of complex processes retains a consultancy which is similarly bureaucratic; or an organisation which communicates through indirectness receives from the consultancy a diagnostic report which is characterised by qualifying, multiple sub-clauses (some in brackets)!

To reduce the chances of this happening, the coaching team needs to be aware of its collective personality and idiosyncrasies. It must grapple with its 'shadow side' – *'what are we really like at our worst?'*. This exploration is not a luxury, but a necessity. It is the team equivalent of the individual coach ensuring, as best he can, that his personal history does not inappropriately intrude into the coaching relationship. How can a coaching team hope to be effective in helping an organisation deal with self-defeating behaviours if it is not aware of its own? The earlier point about training and development is relevant here since it reduces the chances of an unhelpful mind-set being created. It also might mean that the manager of coaches should not also be the coaching supervisor. This could be better done, perhaps, by an outsider - indeed maybe even somebody with whom the team does not feel totally comfortable; this person might bring value through challenging underlying assumptions and habits.

To summarise, the coaching team needs to contract well internally, in order to contract well externally with the client organisation. In doing so, the team is more likely to have clear boundaries for its work. This is important because the client organisation is sometimes a difficult and confusing place where the boundaries are quite fuzzy, sometimes seductively so. Organisational politics, lack of a clear business strategy and conflicting roles can make coaching more necessary but, paradoxically, also more difficult to carry out.

If the coaching team has to work hard to maintain a clear perspective, then, arguably, the challenge is even greater for the coachee's manager who, almost by definition, is more deeply embedded in the organisation. We consider this in the next chapter.

on occasions one can mentally rehearse a conversation so many times, one almost ends up believing it has already taken place

chapter six

Perspectives – the coachee's manager

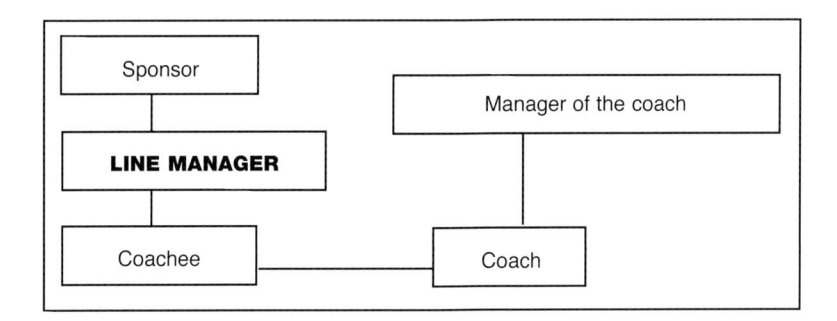

```
┌─────────────────────────────────────────────────┐
│  ┌──────────┐                                   │
│  │ Sponsor  │        ┌────────────────────┐     │
│  └────┬─────┘        │ Manager of the coach│    │
│       │              └──────────┬─────────┘     │
│  ┌────┴─────────┐               │               │
│  │ LINE MANAGER │               │               │
│  └────┬─────────┘               │               │
│       │                         │               │
│  ┌────┴─────┐          ┌────────┴──┐            │
│  │ Coachee  │──────────│   Coach   │            │
│  └──────────┘          └───────────┘            │
└─────────────────────────────────────────────────┘
```

Another vital presence, whether literally or not, in the coaching room is the coachee's line manager; as such he or she can be a positive or negative influence. The line manager has the opportunity, regardless of whether taking the coaching role or not, to integrate coaching into staff management and development. In this chapter we describe how this might happen.

The versatility of coaching, both in its form and content, means that the line manager can use it in many different ways. It can often be moulded to take into account the prevailing climate and processes as well as opening up many exciting new possibilities. The line manager may well be a central figure in this, should she or he choose to be so.

LINE MANAGER AS COACH?

An immediate consideration is whether the line manager is also the coach. If the coaching is part of a performance management process then it is likely that this is the case.

If there are choices to be made about whether the line manager should be the coach, then there are points to be made for and against:

- The line manager may be available for 'ad hoc' coaching and indeed may initiate coaching on the basis of direct observation; immediacy can be a significant benefit. However, the coaching session may, because of the very fact of its immediacy, be hurried, focusing on feedback and quick fixes rather than helping the coachee develop her own solutions. In being part of that local culture the coachee may have low expectations, simply equating being coached with being told what to do.

- In a coaching role the line manager may be well placed to adjust the coachee's responsibilities to accommodate points emerging, from the coaching; for example, he can offer more challenging work if that is appropriate.

- The line manager may lose perspective as a coach because of having too strong an investment in the coachee's performance. This might be exacerbated (*'I feel under even more pressure now'*), or alleviated (*'I can get help with this'*) if the line manager's own performance is partly assessed by the amount and quality of coaching delivered. One of the warning signs is if the line manager takes the coachee's poor performance personally. However, this can still happen even when the line manager is not also the coach.

- The line manager may be well equipped to handle skills coaching. If however the coachee's needs are more around life, and possibly even performance, then a third party coach, from inside or outside the organisation, might be more helpful. The coachee's need for confidentiality may be greater and she might, understandably, feel very uncomfortable confiding in her boss. In certain situations it might be difficult for the line manager to make a commitment to confidentiality where an individual's performance is under detailed scrutiny; there may, for example, be a suspicion that the coachee has been bullying others, or not handling part of her role ethically.

- If the line manager is also the coach there is a greater risk of the ad hoc session becoming too informal; it may be a casual conversation which drifts into coaching. When a third party undertakes the coaching there is more likely to be preparation and rigour almost automatically built in – especially if there is money involved; this can concentrate the mind wonderfully! However, there will obviously be many line managers who are extremely meticulous and disciplined about their staff coaching responsibilities.

A partnership. Two other aspects which are worth mentioning briefly. One is the possibility of the coaching line manager, the third party coach and the coachee all working in partnership. It can be highly successful if the parameters are clear; the line manager coaches on a day-to-day basis, with the external coach coming in regularly to review and consolidate, possibly also dealing with more personal issues. We would suggest that the coachee should always be the channel of communication between the coaches and that there are regular, three-way meetings. Any other approach risks misunderstandings and accusations of breach of confidentiality.

Peer coaching. The other aspect is the possibility of peer coaching. This is where colleagues coach each other. It can have several advantages. First, the coaching may happen more immediately than if the line manager were to be involved. Secondly, it can reduce any problems of rank that might have existed if the line manager were coaching. Thirdly, it can be developmental for both coach and coachee, as well as possibly building the team. A word of caution, however, is that the line manager should not expect to reduce his involvement immediately. There is some careful preparation to be done in establishing the parameters, and making the roles and responsibilities clear. As such it is no different from any other delegated project. Our impression is that peer coaching is most often directed towards specific skills needs, but this is not necessarily so.

RAISING THE NEED FOR COACHING

There will be many occasions when the coachee does not initiate the coaching. The prompt will often come from the line manager. The line manager thus needs to create the conditions where the coachee is willing to take the first step on the journey. What must be considered here involves the well-established territory of giving and receiving feedback; we will not visit this in detail, but refer briefly to some key elements.

Challenging performance. One line of approach is particularly evident if the coaching is set in the context of performance management. We are then concerned with what is commonly referred to as 'challenging performance'. In order to do this, the line manager will probably have certain actions to take; first, gathering the specific evidence about performance, and secondly, considering whether there might be other factors affecting the person's performance (for example, a change in the pattern or flow of work into the office). This might also lead to an investigation of whether the performance of other staff has also fallen away. From these considerations, the line manager might then be led into other areas when looking for possible solutions. These may include group coaching, work process revisions and perhaps negotiating new arrangements with a supplier.

In this setting of 'challenging performance' the line manager might well want to reflect on which particular aspect of performance he wants to raise; for example the most important one, or the one which is perhaps more easily and quickly improved. There is then the 'when, where and how' of approaching the staff member - setting the tone, keeping it simple, avoiding interruptions, allowing sufficient time. Sometimes the line manager might believe that he has raised this issue already, but in fact has not really done so – a passing comment has been made, but this does not necessarily mean that the person heard it or realised its significance. On occasions one can mentally rehearse a conversation so many times one almost ends up believing it has already taken place!

Another approach just as valid, but perhaps less well documented, is the use of intuition. An example of this may be noticing that the person's performance is as good as ever, but that he has 'lost some of his sparkle', or that he is making one or two minor, but uncharacteristic mistakes. Here the very first step, which might eventually lead to coaching, could simply be the words, *'are you OK?'*.

Fostering the right environment. The aim for the line manager may well be to foster an environment where the initiating of coaching, no matter by whom, is of no great significance; it is simply the 'way we do things round here'. The line manager can greatly contribute to this through his management style, encouraging such activities as self-assessment and peer reviews.

CONTRIBUTOR TO A LEARNING ORGANISATION – THE INFLUENCE OF THE ENVIRONMENT

In considering the role of the line manager in coaching we are immediately taken to two questions, which have been core to management development literature for several decades. These questions are *'what, if any, are the manager's responsibilities for staff development?'* and *'how should they be carried out?'*.

The debate around these questions has, at least in part, centred on the concept of the 'learning organisation'. That is, the prosperity and long-term health of the business is dependent upon the continuous up-grading of the talent of its members. To achieve this, priority has to be given to learning from and with colleagues – regardless of 'rank' - and from those outside the organisation – customers, suppliers, competitors and the wider community. Within such a 'world view', coaching sits comfortably, being an activity which can evidently support mutual learning. Equally evident is the fact that there are many organisations that are not run on such a basis, and indeed have no aspirations in this direction. Here, skills are brought in rather than developed internally; there is little, if any, attempt to learn from successes or failures; people are 'empowered', and then potentially disempowered when the share price falls; those who question underlying assumptions – an activity vital for learning - are labelled 'difficult'. Of course, reality is not usually quite so stark as this. The distinction can be blurred by the existence of a local manager who steadfastly encourages staff development despite the prevailing culture, or the fact that the performance management system has not degenerated into 'ticks in boxes'. It may be that the arrival of a new chief executive – committed and articulate – suddenly breathes new life into an organisation which was in danger of reframing the mediocre as satisfactory.

So, into this picture – simple or complex, clear or confused, nourishing or suffocating – steps the line manager. Narrowing the focus again to coaching again we can see that the culture may be supportive, neutral or (despite protestations to the contrary) hostile. We suggest that the line manager might have a similar range of attitudes – supportive *'I really believe coaching has an important role to play in staff development and am keen to play my part'*, neutral *'I am not totally convinced of the value of coaching, but I am open to learning about it and then decide'*, and hostile *'I am opposed to taking on any coaching responsibilities because it distracts me from meeting my targets and our real business – but of course I am careful to whom I say that!'*.

We combine these standpoints in figure six, suggesting an appropriate stance for the line manager:

Figure six
Attitudes to coaching

```
                    Line manager
                     supportive
                         ↑
     Maximise the       │      Create room for
       benefits         │        manoeuvre
                        │
                    ┌───────┐
Organisation        │       │      Organisation
 supportive  ←──────│Neutral│─────→   hostile
                    │       │
                    └───────┘
                        │
    Avoid getting in    │       Stop the
       the way          │       pretence
                         ↓
                    Line manager
                      hostile
```

Let us consider figure six quadrant by quadrant.

The 'Stop the pretence' quadrant: Where both the line manager and the organisation are hostile about coaching, it seems pointless that the topic should even be discussed. Maybe staff development is seen as a distraction rather than a necessity, or perhaps coaching as a method is not seen as having value? Either way it would seem wasteful to go through the motions, perhaps raising expectations unfairly, the dashing of which then becomes a further distraction.

The 'Avoid getting in the way' quadrant: This situation arises fairly often when an organisation goes through some major changes, perhaps from command and control to collaboration, but the line manager has not adapted. We suggest that this person in this situation, in the short term, even if it is only for reasons of politics and self-preservation, allows others to get involved in coaching. In the longer term, his position is probably untenable, particularly if coaching is becoming central to how the organisation does business. So this particular line manager might consider a number of options including being willing to learn more about coaching or even getting trained in some of the basic skills. Of course, ultimately the line manager might consider looking for a different organisation.

The 'Create room for manoeuvre' quadrant: This is familiar territory for a lot of managers. It means finding a way of operating in spite of the organisation. Often these pragmatic manoeuvrings contribute greatly to business results – like cutting through internal bureaucracy to help a customer. However, they carry with them a risk of being marginalized for having 'broken the rules'. Relating specifically to coaching, this quadrant may require the coach to have a certain generosity of spirit, since he may well not be receiving coaching himself, at least not from his manager. Indeed he may well decide to coach himself (for example, using the framework described in appendix two), whilst looking for a coach inside or outside the organisation. He may also, over time, choose to accumulate evidence of the value of coaching as a basis for arguing a case for 'cultural change'. The versatility of coaching is that it need not necessarily be a high profile event. A regular and disciplined ten minutes can be very productive, for example asking the coachee to prepare some success criteria prior to a sales meeting. These criteria can then be used for self assessment supported by feedback, as well as forming the basis for agreeing action points. These might relate to some guided reading or to sitting in on another colleague's sales visit. Arguably, this relates to good management practice, plain and simple. It is crucial in this quadrant that the manager is proactive and is not trapped into believing that he cannot coach unless he 'gets permission' from the organisation. Otherwise he could be in for a very long wait.

The 'Maximise the benefits' quadrant: This may well give the line manager the opportunity to develop coaching into some particularly interesting and valuable areas. One aspect might be the development of others as coaches, for example to enhance the coaching capabilities within the team. Also, as already touched on, the line manager might want to consider setting up peer coaching with other groups, inside or outside the organisation. This, for example, can be an excellent way of identifying and sharing best practice.

CONTRIBUTOR TO A LEARNING ORGANISATION – LEARNING TO LEARN

This leads us to another important area, the blend of 'content' and 'process' coaching. Content coaching is about learning, process coaching is about learning how to learn.

So far in this book we have implicitly concentrated on content coaching. So some of the relevant questions will be the familiar ones of *'what did you do? ... how successful were you?... what helped and hindered?... what have you learned?... what will you do next time?... how will you do it?...'* The coachee is invited to reflect on his particular area of concern and take action.

Process coaching is designed to help the coachee understand the process he went through in order to learn. The rationale is the assumption that helping the client achieve this 'higher order' of learning will aid transferability; he not only learns, for example, how to handle a difficult customer, but also to handle some other, similar, yet different situations about which he is worried. This level of learning is well documented in Argyris and Schon's seminal book[4]. Thinking about using coaching as a way of getting people to reflect on how they learn is an exciting prospect. It clearly supports self development and gives people the propensity not only to solve today's problems but to become better equipped at handling tomorrow too.

So if we were to do process coaching, some of the questions we might ask could include, *'we now know what you learnt, how did you let yourself be open to learning this?... what skills and qualities have you needed to draw on?... how can you apply these elsewhere?... how, if at all, did you impede your learning?... how, specifically did others help or hinder your learning?... how did you react?... in what ways have I been effective or ineffective as a coach for you?... do you wish you had reacted differently to me?... if so, how?... are there any lessons for you as a learner?... what I have learned is...what is your view?... do you think you have preferred ways of learning?... does coaching support your learning preference?... are there other methods which might be more helpful?... what are your first thoughts on how you might help other members of the team learn?... is that of interest to you?'*

These questions invite the client to take an additional step back from his experience.

---

[4] *C. Argyris and D Schon. 'Organisational Learning: A Theory of Action Perspective'. Addison-Wesley*

Figure seven below illustrates first, that content and process coaching can take place equally in skills, performance and life coaching; secondly, that there is scope for combining content and process coaching, with the blend being almost infinitely variable. On this latter

Figure seven
Content and process coaching

Content coaching

Life

Performance

Skills

Process coaching

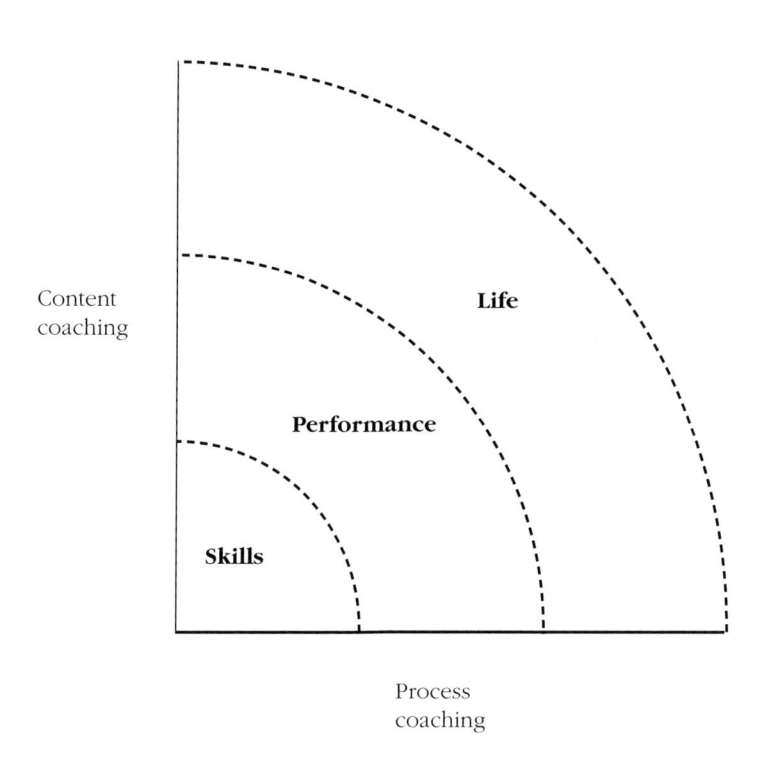

point, a rough guideline might be that in the early stages of the coaching relationship, content coaching predominates. Then, over time, process coaching increases as the coachee becomes an 'aware learner'. In the final stages, process coaching might have the greater prominence since it supports the coachee's independence. It might be the coach's 'parting gift' to the coachee.

If the potential of content coaching has scarcely been tapped in most organisations, then this is even more true of process coaching. A number of factors may influence decisions regarding the extent to which process coaching takes place. First, as already touched on, there is the matter of the general climate in the organisation. If the idea of 'learning how to learn' has widespread currency then process coaching can more easily fit into existing business practice; for example, in the formulation of personal development plans. Secondly, process coaching can often require a higher degree of openness than would typify content coaching. So both coach and coachee need to decide if they are willing to proceed on the basis of the possible greater risk that can accompany such openness. In this it is important for the coach in particular to remember that it is possible to 'test the water'. This could be done simply through introducing just one or two process coaching questions. There is also the possibility of practising these skills with peers, perhaps in a self development group.

Ultimately, with coaching, as with many of the other challenges faced by line managers, it is a matter of posing oneself some critical questions: *'what do I believe in?... what, for me, is the right thing to do?... where do I want to push or conform?... what am I willing to offer?... do I need help?... how will I know if I am making progress?'*

Any certainties which emerge from such questions then provide the solid ground for coaching and supporting others in being coaches.

In this chapter we have described the ways in which the line manager can contribute to creating and sustaining a coaching culture in his organisation. Another figure, often central to that endeavour, is the sponsor. It is that role we consider in the next chapter.

Perspectives – the coachee's manager

*Entering the client's world
but not becoming
absorbed by it*

chapter seven

Perspectives – the sponsor

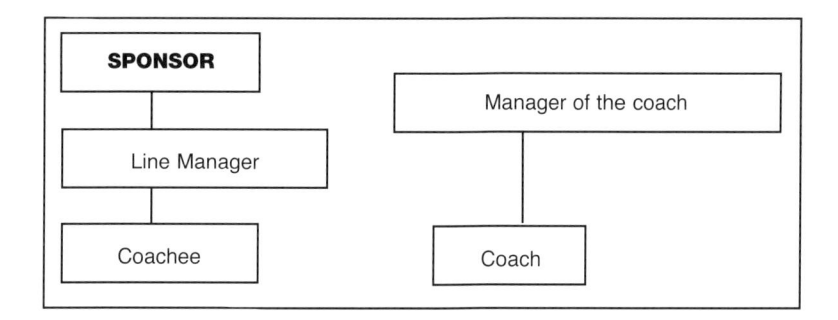

```
┌─────────────────────────────────────────────────┐
│  ┌──────────┐                                   │
│  │ SPONSOR  │         ┌────────────────────┐    │
│  └────┬─────┘         │ Manager of the coach│   │
│       │               └──────────┬─────────┘    │
│  ┌────┴─────┐                    │              │
│  │Line Manager│                  │              │
│  └────┬─────┘                    │              │
│       │               ┌──────────┴─────────┐    │
│  ┌────┴─────┐         │       Coach        │    │
│  │ Coachee  │         └────────────────────┘    │
│  └──────────┘                                   │
└─────────────────────────────────────────────────┘
```

In contrast to the line manager, the sponsor is sometimes a figure who is more in the background. She may, for example, more generally be the creator of the conditions where coaching can take place in the organisation. In this chapter we examine the many manifestations of this role and suggest that positioning and clarity of purpose are essential if the organisation is to derive maximum benefit from any investment it makes in coaching.

For many sponsors a major benefit of coaching is that it need not be 'all or nothing'. In other words, its very richness makes it amenable to a 'step by step' approach, with the sponsor being in a strong position to test and monitor reactions, adapting strategy and tactics as needed.

As previously mentioned, the sponsor is the person who puts her authority behind the coaching taking place. Depending on the circumstances – which as we know can vary hugely – the sponsor could, for example, be the line manager authorising payment for an external coach to give a staff member a one-off session on presentation skills; equally the sponsor could be the human resources director launching a company-wide coaching initiative designed to spearhead 'culture change'. So the responsibilities may be relatively confined or highly extensive. Figure eight below maps out in very broad terms the possible areas where sponsorship may be involved.

Let us consider the figure in some detail. The 'point of emphasis' dimension relates to the main thrust of the coaching. It may concentrate on individual, team or organisation development. The 'approach' dimension indicates that an initiative may either be localised, happening in a piecemeal way, or linked, drawing together various needs and themes.

Figure eight

Focus of sponsorship in coaching

Point of Emphasis

Approach

	Individual development	Team development	Organisation development
Localised	Coaching prompted by local initiative – usually coachee/line manager. Takes place randomly as needed. The arrangements are made locally – timing, length of coaching sessions, objectives, review.	Arranged as need arises: 1:1 coaching to support a team building event. Coaching for a few selected groups, for example actual or potential fast-track staff; induction of new staff; technical specialists moving into staff management role.	Ad hoc initiatives – raising awareness through training, learning resource materials. General promoting of coaching as 'a good thing'.
Linked	Plan for all staff to have a coach. Making coaching an integral part of staff development. There are general policies/guidelines about what should happen – who initiates; frequency of sessions; links, if any, with appraisal, personal development plans.	Plan for all teams to have team events as a matter of routine. There may be an arrangement for 1:1 coaching to support the team event. Plan for all teams to be coached. May be a focus on improving inter-team communication.	Strategic plan building on individual and team coaching. Integrated into other change projects. Marketing of the initiative together with clear guidance on how the process will unfold. May be designed to support cultural integration (for example, after mergers and acquisitions).

With this figure in mind, we want to highlight several points:

First, as the dotted lines indicate, it is possible, sometimes even desirable, to move from one area to another. For example, a coachee receives some very effective coaching ('localised/individual development'), and the decision is made to offer this more formally to other staff (moving towards 'linked/individual development'). We would obviously urge the sponsor to be alert to such shifts, because they can sometimes happen almost with a momentum of their own. This may well be very positive, tapping into people's curiosity and enthusiasm. However, the sponsor may find herself responsible for what has become a project in which she has little interest. Equally she may need more support, and indeed need more sponsors in order to influence the growing number of stakeholders. There may also be a need to develop coping strategies for handling those who were originally obstructive but now want to lay claim to an increasingly significant and successful initiative! So sponsors can become victims of their own success, spreading themselves too thinly in the organisation and losing focus. This is a phenomenon which has strong parallels with what can happen when a coach allows herself to be overloaded.

Secondly, if the point of emphasis moves away from individual to organisational development then there is a shift towards trying to create what is commonly called a 'coaching culture'. The assumption is that, in today's business environment, there is a vital need for flexibility, proactivity, sharing of best practice and partnership with customers. In such a culture, authority is based on knowledge and skill, not rank. Coaching is seen as a way of helping develop, refine and maintain these capabilities. In spearheading such a shift, the challenge for the sponsor is often about putting enough structure around the initiatives – so that they all pull in the same direction – but ensuring that the structure does not stifle local enthusiasm and flexibility.

Thirdly, whatever the focus for the coaching, the sponsor is potentially a powerful role model. Whether line manager or human resources director, that person will be under scrutiny to see whether she also is willing to be coached. There can be few excuses for the sponsor refusing to take part!

Fourthly, if the coaching has high visibility, the sponsor may well want to 'load experiments for success'[5] to begin with. For example, she might want to make sure that initially only positive and motivated people are coached; that the emphasis is developmental rather than remedial.

As we have seen, the effectiveness of the coach is dependent upon entering the coachee's world but not becoming absorbed by it. The sponsor has a similar challenge in relating to those parts of the organisation she is seeking to influence. She needs to acknowledge

---

[5] *Herb Shepard. 'Rules of Thumb for Change Agents' in 'Organisation Development and Transformation', ed. French et al. McGraw-Hill.*

concern and capture excitement, but retain a clarity of purpose which does not become a symbol of either arrogance or subservience. Part of this challenge is also to build bridges with other individuals or groups who can inform and perhaps transform the coaching. As with many change initiatives the process is as important as the content. For example, meetings and debate about coaching may end up being as influential as the coaching itself.

So far we have been emphasising variety and difference. Nevertheless, whatever the focus for the coaching, there will be some basics that always need to be in place: confidentiality (including those aspects which will probably never be treated as confidential – sexism, racism, bullying, fraud, safety), clear ethical standards, clear contracting, personal responsibility, mutual respect, realism, optimism and ongoing willingness to challenge. An illustration of the last point is that sponsors often find it necessary to probe a line manager who is requesting coaching for a member of his staff. The line manager may, underneath it all, be avoiding responsibility for challenging performance, or hoping that the coaching will provide a pretext for eventually getting rid of the staff member. He wants to be able to say, *'well I did my best for them......';* this has shades of tokenism. It can then undermine, in the longer term, the credibility of coaching in the organisation.

The sponsor will also need to be alert to those situations where the line manager is a poor role model. We know of a clever and autocratic national sales director of a domestic appliance company who wanted his regional sales managers to be much more effective in 'kerbside coaching' – that is de-briefing sales representatives after visits to retailers. Whilst wanting this coaching to be much more focused on listening, the national sales director was fairly and necessarily challenged by the sponsor who said, *'the truth of it is that you are not a good listener yourself. Are you willing to change your behaviour to support this initiative? If you do not it will not work.'*.

Along with a good knowledge of what is really going on in the organisation, the sponsor will want to be well-briefed on other resources and mechanisms which can support coaching: peer support, secondments, formal education and training, rewards, promotion, expanded or redefined roles. Change, whether individual or organisational, usually needs to be approached from a variety of directions.

So, whilst taking what are, apparently, very different roles, the core issues for the coach and sponsor will be very similar. We summarise and illustrate this by considering the perspectives of both the coach and the sponsor of organisation development coaching in figure nine.

Perspectives – the sponsor

Figure nine **Issues for coach and sponsor**

ISSUE	COACH	COACHING SPONSOR
RESPONSIBILITY	How much effort am I willing to put into helping the coachee change? How can I help establish the conditions where the coachee takes action?	How much effort am I willing to put into helping the organisation change? How can I help establish the conditions where others are proactive, take action, experiment, follow up?
SUPPORT	Where can I get the support I need to be as effective as possible in helping the coachee?	What people/processes do I need to have in place so that I am sufficiently supported?
CLARITY	How much clarity do I need to have about the desired end point before the coaching begins? Can I use the coaching to create that clarity?	Who are the stakeholders I need to talk to in order to get clarity about the desired future of the organisation?
LEVERAGE	What are the existing processes, reward systems, development resources available that I can use to support/motivate the coachee to change?	What other change mechanisms, in addition to coaching, are at my disposal? How can I best avoid over selling?
CREATIVITY	How can I maintain a freshness of approach, which will support the client in being open to new possibilities?	How can I encourage contributions from others who may have some novel perspectives? How can I design reviews to be dynamic processes encouraging new ideas?
HONESTY	How can I ensure that the coaching is a safe place where each of us is really open about what is helping/hindering progress?	How can I gather around me colleagues who will be truly simple and straightforward about our progress, or lack of it?
OPTIMISM	How can I maintain a positive frame of mind, avoiding blaming myself or the coachee if we hit 'sticky patches'. For example, if the coachee feels really stuck how can I make sure I see it as a signal that there are some vital issues to explore?	How can I maintain a positive frame of mind so that, for example, challenges to the change strategy really are opportunities to learn and re-adjust or re-affirm the vision?
RISK	How can I maintain appropriate challenge in my coaching so that the coachee learns when moving out of his/her 'comfort zone'?	How do I select the challenge I present and to whom? Where are my castles (places to think / recuperate) and battlefields (openly confront / push)?
TIMING	When will the coachee be most receptive to my feedback? Is now the time to sit quietly?	Have the initiatives enough momentum for me to pull back? Is it the right time to widen involvement, or will that confuse the situation?

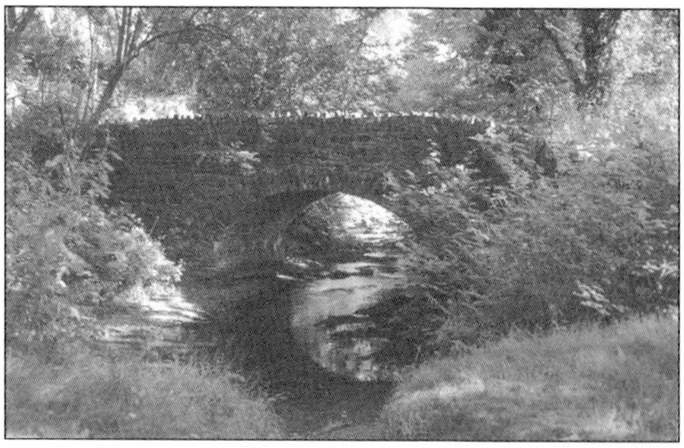

Perspectives – the sponsor

Sometimes the sponsor is a strong reflector of the organisation's culture. They both have similar strengths and weaknesses. If so, the sponsor might well want to reflect on three points. First, with which, if any, of the issues set out in figure nine she really struggles, since this might indicate that this is a more general obstacle to promoting coaching in the organisation. Secondly, what are the issues which she automatically assumes, almost without thinking, are not a problem. This is to consider possible 'blind spots' in the organisation which are based on a collective, but misplaced faith, that certain features can be taken for granted. For example, there may be an automatic assumption that there is a clearly understood business strategy or that the appraisal scheme has high credibility. Thirdly, to consider which, if any, of the issues are 'undiscussable'. As Chris Argyris described it in his article on 'Skilled Incompetence'[6] there are often aspects of an organisation which people do not allow themselves to discuss and their undiscussability itself cannot be discussed. So is there an issue which, if the sponsor raised it, would 'really put the cat amongst the pigeons'?

Perhaps the sponsor would do well to employ the equivalent of Lear's Fool; someone who, with humorous simplicity, has the courage to tell her the truth as he sees it. All too often in today's business world, such honesty is not always welcomed.

We have seen in this chapter that the sponsor of coaching has many manifestations. She may be central or peripheral, have a high or low profile and be responsible for a few individuals or the whole organisation. Her business environment may be equally variable. With this in mind, we would encourage any sponsor of coaching to award herself the luxury and necessity of time to reflect. What does she really want to achieve in sponsoring coaching and does her role permit her to make this happen?

We now move on to our conclusions.

---

[6] *C. Argyris. 'Skilled Incompetence'. Harvard Business Review. Vol 64, No 5.*

*think globally
act locally*

chapter eight

Conclusion

Coaching is a versatile tool which can contribute much to individual and organisational effectiveness. It has many manifestations and that is part of its strength. It can happen simply on the basis of a single manager taking a small, but significant initiative; equally, it can be central to a large-scale change programme. This versatility is the key to its vitality, without which those essential qualities of creativity, individual and collective responsibility and sensitivity to customer need, will not be nurtured. So if, as seems likely, the use of coaching continues to accelerate, the challenge for all of us will be to remember that no tool has, of itself, an inherent virtue; it depends on the use to which it is put. With this in mind, we borrow a catchphrase from the environmental movement: 'Think globally, act locally'.

What does 'think globally, act locally' mean for coaching? We suggest this means, first, retain a wider view of the types of organisation we want to help create and the ethical foundations which must be there to support them; secondly, remember that each coaching session is an opportunity to strengthen those foundations.

In conclusion therefore, we suggest that coaching is, by definition, concerned with change. This change may be motivated by feelings ranging from a sense of crisis to mild unease. Similarly, any of the stakeholders may be driven by a need to stabilise and improve a performance in decline, or a desire to enhance what is already excellent. As figure ten below indicates, creating positive change is based on balancing three themes:

Generating awareness of the present. That is, considering such questions as, *'what assumptions and beliefs govern my behaviour?... what delights and disappoints me in terms of my own performance and that of others?... what opportunities are open to me and my colleagues?... who and what are the real assets and liabilities of our business?'*.

Acknowledging the past. That is, considering such questions as, *'what progress have I and others made?... how has history shaped me and my organisation?'... what, if any, is the legacy of old alliances and conflicts?... and are there traditions to be honoured, or relinquished or both?'.*

Nurturing aspirations for the future. That is, considering such questions as, *'what will characterise the commitments I am willing to make to myself and my organisation?... how can I ensure I continue to be open to possibilities?... what ideals will underpin the business over the longer term?'.*

Figure ten
Creating positive change

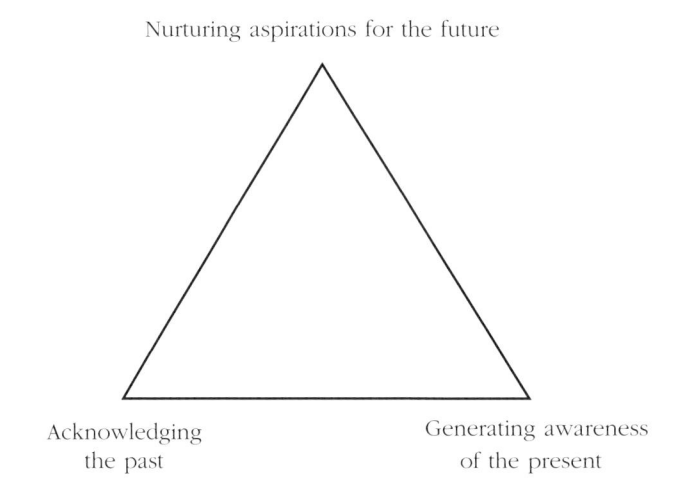

```
                Nurturing aspirations for the future
                              /\
                             /  \
                            /    \
                           /      \
                          /        \
                         /          \
                        /_____\
           Acknowledging          Generating awareness
             the past                of the present
```

At any point in time the emphasis with these themes may vary, depending on the needs of the individual and the organisation. Coaching is a way of identifying those needs, how they match and mismatch, and finding the points of resolution.

In this book we have tried to give an overview of coaching, bringing to it the immediacy of our own experiences, pleasurable, occasionally painful and sometimes confusing. Our faith in organisational coaching has not only been confirmed, in writing this book, but we have the added delight of seeing even more possibilities that we had previously imagined. Our journey continues.....

Conclusion

balancing permission and protection

Appendices

APPENDIX ONE – THE CONTRACT IN COACHING

The importance of good contracting is that it offers, borrowing and adapting a phrase from the world of therapy, 'permission and protection'[7]. In other words, an agreement about the freedom to explore, but within clearly defined limits. The word contracting has a legalistic ring to it, which can be misleading in the world of coaching since it should not lead to confrontations about the meaning of words or, except in very rare circumstances, the seeking of redress. There is, however, some similarity since the parties can hold each other to account – this then being used to clarify further roles and expectations.

There are two main levels to contracting – technical and psychological. Neither is more important than the other and, indeed, each can support the other.

The technical contract is the more obvious. Much of it may well be in written form, especially if the coach is an external provider. It is likely to cover such aspects as: the broad focus of the work; the length, frequency and location of meetings; confidentiality, what sort of information will be shared, if at all, and with whom; mechanisms for reviewing progress; arrangements for any contact between sessions; agreements on how cancellations are to be handled and, where appropriate, fees. The coach might also declare the ethical guidelines that she/he will commit to follow. The spirit of these 'technical' discussions is an exchange of wants and needs, with each party being alert to those aspects they regard as non-negotiable.

It is highly likely that in dealing with these technical aspects, the psychological level of contracting will have already started: the testing out of trust, the gathering sense, or otherwise, of competence and the early exploration of openness. There may also be some patterns emerging in terms of risk taking and challenge. Much of this is likely to be implicit in the early stages (in contrast to the technical) but may well be brought to the surface, by coach or coachee as the coaching progresses. So psychological contracting is much more evolutionary, developing as the relationship grows. It is very important that, as issues arise,

---

[7] *P Crossman 'Permission and Protection'. Transactional Analysis Bulletin 5 No 19, 1966*

the coach takes responsibility for making them explicit as different views on the nature of the psychological contract can have major repercussions. In other words, the coach treats the relationship between himself and the coachee as a fundamental topic for both parties to review regularly.

It is quite often said that coaching contracts are made between equals. Whilst acknowledging this inherent truth, it is important not to be blind to some crucial differences. First, the needs are not equal in the coaching room. The coach is there to help the coachee. The coach cannot, indeed should not, expect to be helped with her/his needs, or only to the extent that there is some underlying purpose related to coachee needs. For example, the coach might say, '*I need you to keep to your agreement about writing a diary between sessions so that I can more effectively help you review progress.*'.

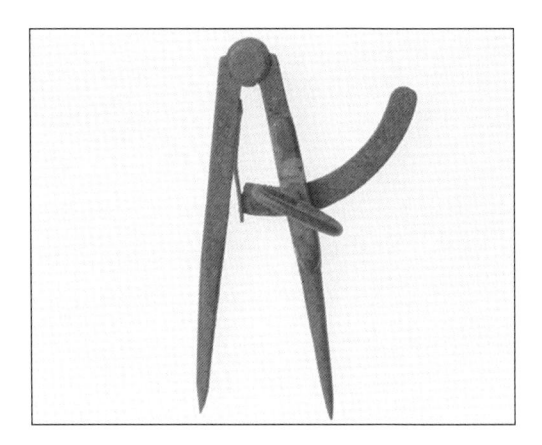

Secondly, the coachee may not have had previous experience of coaching and cannot truly know to what she is agreeing. She needs the coaching actually to have started before being able to make a considered and informed judgement about it.

These aspects reinforce the paradox that the contract is both firm and provisional. How these unfold, and the interplay of the technical and psychological, will ultimately depend on a totally unique and personal process as these two people find a way of working together.

There will often be more than two parties to the contract; the coachee's line manager, the coach's manager and the sponsor may all be involved. Good quality and relevant contracting will need to take place with all who have a role to play. The word relevant is important because there may well be different agreements with different people. For example, the coachee may not have any information about, or indeed, interest in the matter of fees. This agreement may only involve the coach and sponsor.

The coach and coachee may establish a psychological contract where both agree that the latter needs to share his underlying fears about work and the organisation. There is no reason to expect that the sponsor or even the coachee's line manager should be similarly revealing.

To avoid later difficulties the coach may well want to make it clear to the sponsor, at an early stage that what goes on between coach and coachee is confidential. Some sponsors implicitly expect the coach to 'spill the beans' and openly give an assessment of the coachee.

When it comes to 'ad hoc' coaching, perhaps a few minutes during the working day, often between the line manager and coachee, then it is easy to assume immediately that what we have written about contracting has much less relevance. We would suggest that even here there is a need for some clear agreements about the when, where and how of the coaching, and the psychological relationship needed to support it.

APPENDIX TWO – A FRAMEWORK FOR SESSION MANAGEMENT

Below is a framework which the coach might use to shape the overall direction of a coaching session and a set of prompt questions that might be useful. It assumes that the initial relationship and contract have been established.

It is important to remember that the stages listed are not mutually exclusive but have simply been teased apart to show the point of emphasis; it is iterative not linear. That is, any previous stage may need to be revisited in the light of new information. Not all the stages need to be completed in one session, and obviously the needs of the client will ultimately determine the pace of the work. We invite the coach to approach this framework as master, not servant.

Targeting – Identifying what the need is and what is to be achieved. What is your concern?… How is this problem for you?… Can you give me an example?… What exactly happened?… How do you think I might help?… What are you feeling?… What outcome are you looking for?… What would success look like?

Exploring – Considering the context and whether there are other issues which could require the desired outcome to be revised. What else is happening?… Have there been any important changes lately?… What actions have you already taken?… Have you talked to anybody else about this?… What did they say?… Does the outcome we talked about at the beginning still seem relevant/desirable/achievable?… What do you know/imagine others are saying about this situation?

Focusing – Encouraging the client to identify possible actions. What choices do you have for dealing with this situation?… Have you thought about…..? Looking at it from the perspective of X, would this give you other choices?… What might the consequences be if you were to?… What support might you need?… How might you get it?… Let us do some brainstorming of possible actions.

Deciding – Helping the client make a decision and then testing their commitment to it. Which of the choices is the most attractive?… Let us re-cap and work through the specific actions you will need to take, are you really committed to this?… Is there a part of you that really does not want to do this?… Is there anything else you need to put in place to reinforce your decision?… From what you know about yourself, how might you not follow through with this?… What are your specific time scales?

Reviewing – Planning to follow up. How will you know if you have been successful?… What will be different?… Who will be different?… Whom do you want to involve in reviewing the outcomes?… How will you set that up?… When would be a good time?… Do you want some interim reviews?

Following Up – Helping the client consider the results. What did you do?… What happened?… Bearing in mind what you wanted to achieve, in what ways were you successful/unsuccessful?… Have you discussed the results with others?…. What did they say? What did you feel?… What do you feel about it now?… What is your learning for next time?… How can you build in reminders for success?… How can you best acknowledge your achievement?…What, if anything, will you want from me?

APPENDIX THREE - SUGGESTED GUIDELINES FOR THE COACHEE

1. Find out about the coach's background and training.

2. See whether you can have a 'taster' session.

3. Understand how many sessions you must commit to and how the process can be brought to a close.

4. If you are being 'required' to have coaching, get as much clarity as possible about what is expected of you, talk to your line manager or the sponsor of the initiative.

5. Bring a 'small', but real issue to the first coaching session if you have some doubts about the process.

6. If you are not sure why the coach is suggesting something, then ask. If after the coach's explanation you still do not understand, ask again. Never do something simply because the coach suggests it is a good idea.

7. Do not expect that the coaching will always be simple and easy. The role of the coach is to ask awkward questions from time to time, even regularly. You may come to the end of a coaching session feeling confused, and possibly irritated with the coach. That is not necessarily a bad thing, but do tell the coach.

8. Trust your intuition; if the coach says or does anything about which you feel uneasy, challenge the coach and/or go to a relevant third party.

9. Make sure you have other sources of support so that you do not have too much reliance on the coaching sessions alone for making progress. Coaches have a particular obligation to help you, but they are only human.

10. Consider keeping a diary of your coaching sessions – the main themes, your reaction at the time and afterwards; what you are choosing not to tell the coach. (The coach might suggest you do this anyway).

11. If you feel like ending the process prematurely, this might indicate you are on the verge of a real breakthrough. Always discuss this with your coach and never just walk away.

Appendices

APPENDIX FOUR – TOOLS AND TECHNIQUES

The coach needs to use a range of important skills, including:

- Listening to what the coachee says and how they say it (bored, indifferent, excited, angry, cautious, ambivalent, purposeful).

- Being alert to the 'throw away' comment.

- Challenging inconsistencies or the avoidance of personal responsibility.

- Knowing when not to challenge, even if the coachee is being blatantly inconsistent.

- Knowing when/when not to offer theory.

- Asking concise questions.

- Sitting out silences.

- Offering appreciation and support.

- Apologising simply and without self-justification.

- Framing suggestions so that they are genuine invitations, not thinly masked recommendations.

- Taking risks, whilst respecting the coachee's and one's own limitations.

- Keeping to time.

- Knowing when and how to interrupt.

- Being appropriately self revealing.

- Accepting that ultimately the coachee may or may not choose to make changes.

Appendices

The techniques briefly summarised below can only be seen as supporting good practice and are not a substitute for these core skills.

1. *Asking the coachee to keep a diary.* This might cover events, feelings, themes, significant exchanges (who said what and how). However, the basis of it should be informality and curiosity, with the coachee taking notes of interest. The moment it becomes a burden its value is lost.

2. *Using the coachee's hobbies to develop an alternative perspective.* 'One client was very interested in dance. I encouraged her to experiment with various steps which epitomised her attitude to aspects of her work. She created some new steps to characterise a new approach she might take. Another client loved films – he identified quite strongly with the Michael Douglas character in 'Falling Down' – angry, alienated, hurting those he loved and ultimately self destructive. We explored what it might actually mean for him to mirror that role at work, and what other film characters he might more helpfully identify with. For example, the boy in 'Never-ending Story', who retained his optimism and belief in the inherent goodness of people, despite many temptations to give up – including meeting people who did not care that they did not care!'

3. *Taking different roles.* This is a long-standing technique which originated in the world of psychodrama. The coachee takes it in turn to sit in various chairs which represent the various characters in a situation: for example, boss, customer, colleague. In sitting in each of those chairs, the coachee takes the perspective of that other person. It is often useful to have a 'neutral chair', in which the coachee can sit to consider options for handling the needs/demands/expectations of the other parties. Beware of bringing in too many characters, otherwise it will get very confusing, not least for the coach!

4. *Using different media – pictures, clay, stories.* As we know, words can sometimes get in the way of communication and cloud some simple truths. Asking the coachee, for example, to draw a picture, which summarises the key elements of the problem as they see it, can bring an unexpected clarity. 'I drew a picture of a Christmas tree, which captured the essence of my concerns – expected to sparkle, not getting any nourishment then chucked out'. The analogy or materials can be reworked to identify other options. Suggestion – do not try this out with an unfamiliar sponsor who is having a taster coaching session with you; you might appear too zany and 'off the wall'.

5. *Story boarding.* When something goes wrong for a person in their management of a situation, there is usually a crucial point of decision. Clients may not know exactly when this is. For example, she plans to be more assertive with her boss, she starts well, but somehow 'go off track'. Story boarding means breaking the scene down into detail, frame by frame, just as for a film. *'He said this, then you said that, what exactly happened next?... so it was when he said, he was 'disappointed' in you, that you stopped being assertive? ... what were you feeling? ... what were you thinking? ... how would you re-write the frames? ... how can you make it different for yourself next time?'*

6. *Physical movement.* In some ways we have already dealt with this in some of the earlier techniques. However, we wanted to emphasise that frequently if the coachee, and indeed the coach, feel stuck, then it is frequently reflected by a lack of physical movement in the room. For example, both being still, possibly each mirroring the other; one might even argue that the coach has worked so hard to understand the coachee that a mild hypnotic induction has taken place; it is just that the hypnotist is hypnotised as well! So almost anything that creates some physical movement, carries with it the possibility of movement on the issue. Having a flip chart or white board in the room for either person to use can help, so long as the coach does not keep leaping up to make yet another important point!

7. *Psychometrics and questionnaires.* These can be a relatively safe way of helping the coachee take a fresh look at themselves and their concerns. Amongst the more commonly used are Myers Briggs Type Indicator, (MBTI), Fundamental Interpersonal Relationships Orientation-Behaviour (FIRO-B) and Strength Deployment Inventory (SDI) (See appendix seven).

APPENDIX FIVE - SUGGESTED ETHICAL GUIDELINES FOR THE COACH

1. The coach should stop or get support if he/she is worried about getting out of his/her depth.

2. The coach should make and keep confidentiality agreements. These can only be broken where the issues raised are too serious. That is, actual or potential criminal acts involving child safety, health and safety, bullying, sexism, racism, substance abuse and fraud

3. Coaches should have specialists to whom they can make referrals, such as counsellors, therapists and technical specialists.

4. There should be no sexual relations between the coach and coachee.

5. The coach should keep the relationship professional and keep reviewing the boundaries.

6. The coach will make sure he/she receives regular supervision and training.

7. The administration arrangements regarding fees, times, location and duration should be clearly stated.

8. The coach will agree with the coachee clear arrangements for contact between sessions.

9. If the coach anticipates or sees an actual or possible conflict of interest, this will be raised immediately and clearly with the coachee and other relevant parties.

10. The coach will do his/her best to ensure that she/he is well enough, both physically and emotionally, to work well with the coachee. Should this prove not to be the case either before or during the coaching, the coach will inform the client and agree appropriate action.

11. If the coach deeply disapproves of a coachee's actions, the coach has the right to withdraw immediately and respectfully from the relationship, even if those coachee actions are not illegal.

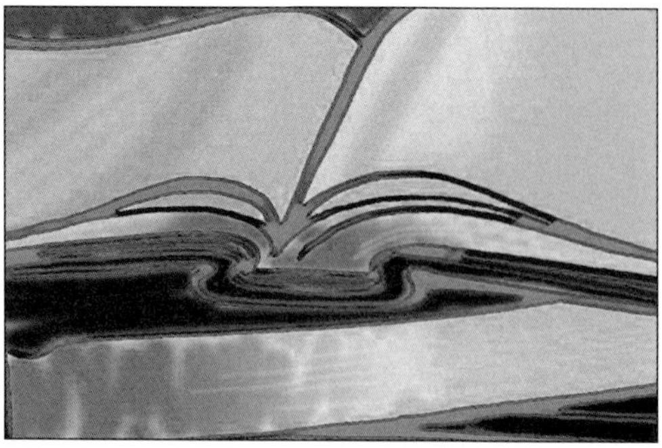

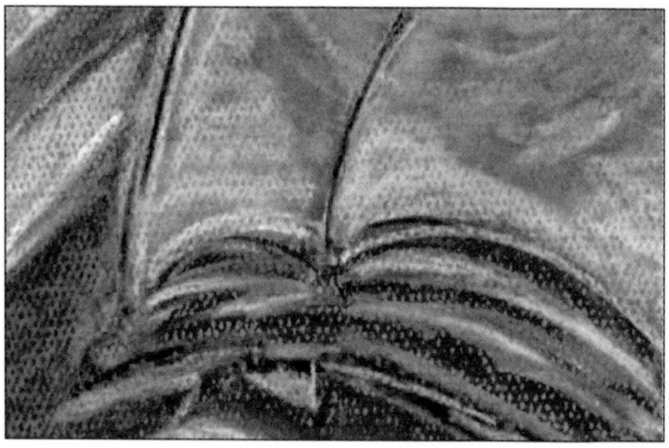

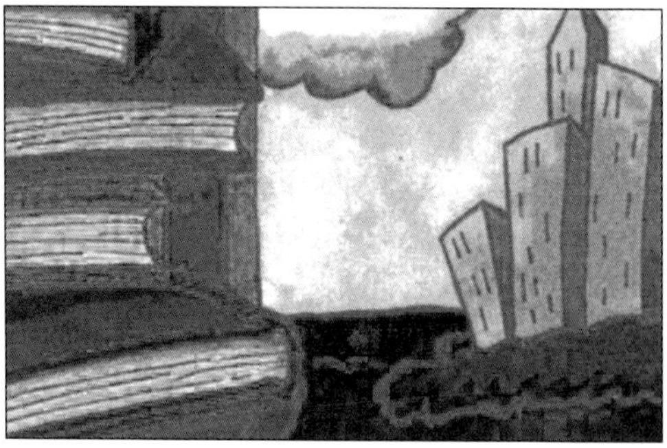

APPENDIX SIX – ANNOTATED BIBLIOGRAPHY

- *Steve Bavister and Amanda Vickers, 'Be Your Best Coach and Beyond', Q Learning, 2003.* A really nice pocket size introductory guide, which coaches the coach on the basics and more.

- *Janice Caplan, 'Coaching for the Future', CIPD. 2003.* A tightly argued text, which covers all the major challenges in introducing coaching and mentoring into organisations. A good blend of theory and principles together with detailed case studies.

- *Jeffrey Kahn and Alan Langlieb, 'Mental Health and Productivity in the Workplace', Jossey Bass. 2003.* This is a wide ranging academic book based on US experience. One of its strengths is its challenge, often implicit, for the reader to consider in depth what is appropriate and relevant in a coaching relationship.

- *Nadine Klasen with David Clutterbuck, 'Implementing Mentoring Schemes', Butterworth-Heinemann, 2002.* A very practical book full of informative detail; particularly helpful on the training that will be necessary.

- *Eric Parsloe and Monika Wray, 'Coaching and Mentoring', Kogan Page, 2000.* Strong on definitions, learning processes and practical guidance.

- *Philippe Rosinski, 'Coaching Across Cultures', Nicholas Brearley 2003.* As the title suggests, particularly strong in exploring cultural differences and the contribution coaching can make in building strength through diversity.

- *J. K. Smart, 'Real Coaching and Feedback', Prentice Hall, 2003.* The theory (always carefully explained) and practice of coaching, particularly viewed through the eyes of the busy manager who has to make every minute count.

- *Julie Starr, 'The Coaching Manual', Prentice Hall, 2003.* If the reader is seeking a detailed guide, with heart, on how to develop and practise as a coach, then it would be hard to find a better book.

- *John Whitmore, 'Coaching for Performance', Nicholas Brearley 2003.*
  Arguably the classic British text on coaching. Originator of the extensively used GROW model – Goal, Reality, Options, Will.

Some other books to consider:

- *Windy Dryden (ed), 'Hard Earned Lessons from Counselling in Action.' Sage. 1995.* A selection of short and graphic stories, which illustrate the significant challenges, mistakes and learning in the experiences of a wide range of counsellors. A potentially rewarding question for the reader is, *'what, if at all, would be equivalent for me in my coaching practice?'*

- *John Heron, 'Helping the Client'. Sage. 2000.* A closely worked and argued book with an extensive range of models for analysing the dynamics of the helping relationship and what may constitute helpful and unhelpful interventions.

- *Richard Nelson-Jones, 'Introduction to Counselling Skills'. Sage. 2003.* A very accessible, reader-focused book, which provides practical suggestions for the development of skills, many of which are highly relevant for the coach. A sophisticated introduction.

- *Irvin Yalom, 'Love's Executioner'. Bloomsbury. 1989.* A delightful and highly personal insight into the work of the psychotherapist. In many ways a refreshing and uplifting antidote to excessive clinical detachment.

Appendices

APPENDIX SEVEN – USEFUL CONTACTS

1. The British Psychological Society has a special interest group on coaching.
   web: www.bps.org.uk
   e-mail: enquiry@bps.org.uk

2. Oxford Psychologists Press provides training, materials and ongoing professional development in MBTI and FIRO-B.
   web: www.opp.co.uk
   e-mail: enquiry@opp.co.uk

3. Emmaus House is a retreat centre offering MBTI training for those in the voluntary sector.
   web: www.emmaus-house.co.uk
   e-mail: emmaushouse@msn.com

4. Coaching Futures offers coaching training to the equivalent of NVQ 4.
   web: www.coachingfutures.co.uk
   e-mail: info@managementfutures.co.uk

5. The International Coach Federation (ICF) offers training, referral and accreditation services. Seen by some as setting the standard. Although US based, it has 'chapters' in other countries including the UK.
   web: www.coachfederation.org
   e-mail : icfoffice@coachfederation.org

6. Association for Coaching is a relatively new organisation offering networking, levels of membership, professional development and open events.
   web: www.associationforcoaching.com
   email: enquiries@associationforcoaching.com

7. Coachville is an informal US based network offering its members an extensive range of coaching materials, shared best practice and advice on setting up a coaching business.
   web: www.coachville.com

8. The Strength Deployment Inventory (SDI) is available to certified users from Personal Strengths Publishing.
   web: www.personalstrength.co.uk

9. Further information on training and development which is available for coaches and mentors:
   web: www.coachingnetwork.org.uk

Final thought

A coaching Haiku:

*I give you focus
and somehow my mere presence
moves you to action*

Phil Lowe

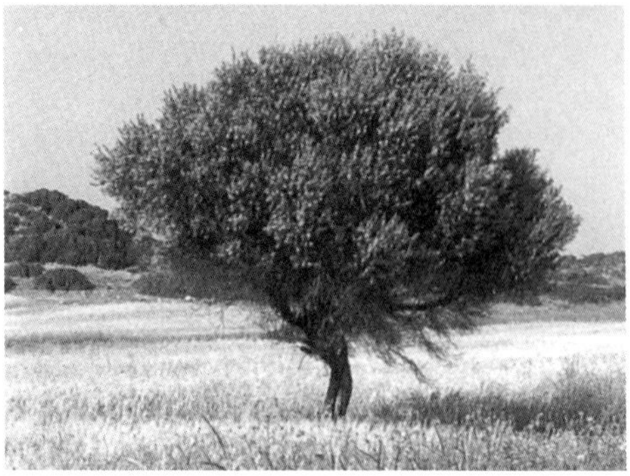